AI FOR SMART KITCHEN

Rakesh Kumar

To Lord Agni, the divine embodiment of fire and hunger, whose presence is felt in every kitchen and whose warmth sustains life itself.

In the depths of our culinary endeavors, we find your sacred essence, guiding our hands as we prepare nourishing meals for ourselves and our loved ones. You are the eternal flame that ignites our passion for cooking and the source of inspiration that fuels our creativity in the kitchen.

As we embark on this journey into the realm of AI for Smart Kitchen, we acknowledge your divine presence, Lord Agni. Just as you reside within each of us as hunger, driving our quest for sustenance, you are also present in the heart of every kitchen, overseeing the alchemical transformation of raw ingredients into delectable dishes.

This book is dedicated to you, Lord Agni, as a tribute to your benevolent presence in our lives and our kitchens. May your sacred fire continue to illuminate our culinary endeavors, guiding us towards greater efficiency, innovation, and sustainability. May we honor your divine essence by embracing the advancements of AI technology to create smarter, more harmonious kitchen environments that nourish both body and soul.

In your eternal flame, we find the warmth of hospitality, the joy of creativity, and the sustenance of life itself. With deepest reverence and gratitude, we dedicate "AI for Smart Kitchen" to you, Lord Agni, as a token of our devotion and appreciation for your timeless presence in our culinary journey.

CONTENTS

INTRODUCTION

In the contemporary era of technological advancement, the integration of Artificial Intelligence (AI) into our daily lives has revolutionized the way we interact with our surroundings. One area that has seen significant transformation is the kitchen – the heart of every home. The convergence of AI and kitchen technology has given rise to the concept of the "Smart Kitchen," where intelligent systems and appliances work harmoniously to enhance efficiency, convenience, and sustainability.

The aim of this book, "AI for Smart Kitchen," is to explore the myriad ways in which AI technologies are reshaping our culinary experiences and revolutionizing the way we interact with our kitchen environments. From automated cooking appliances to personalized recipe suggestions, from predictive inventory management to energy-efficient practices, the possibilities offered by AI in the kitchen are boundless.

In this comprehensive guide, we will delve into the fundamental concepts of AI and its applications in the context of smart kitchens. We will examine the importance and relevance of AI in optimizing kitchen operations, enhancing food quality and safety, and reducing wastage. Through real-world case studies, practical examples, and hands-on tutorials, readers will gain a deep understanding of how AI can transform their culinary routines and elevate their kitchen experiences.

Whether you are a home cook looking to streamline your meal preparation process, a culinary enthusiast eager to explore cutting-edge kitchen technologies, or a professional chef seeking to optimize kitchen operations, this book is your ultimate guide to harnessing the power of AI in the kitchen. Join us on this journey as we unlock the potential of AI for creating smarter, more efficient, and more enjoyable kitchen environments. Welcome to the future of cooking – welcome to the world of AI for Smart Kitchen.

INTRODUCTION TO AI IN THE KITCHEN

In recent years, the integration of artificial intelligence (AI) into various aspects of our daily lives has revolutionized how we interact with technology. One area where AI shows immense promise is in the kitchen. Imagine a kitchen where appliances anticipate your needs, provide personalized recommendations, and streamline everyday tasks. This is the vision of the AI-powered kitchen, where cutting-edge technology enhances efficiency, convenience, and even creativity in cooking and food management.

This book serves as a comprehensive guide to understanding and harnessing the power of AI in the kitchen. Whether you're a seasoned chef, a busy parent, or someone simply looking to simplify meal preparation and improve your culinary experience, this book is designed to provide valuable insights into the potential of AI-driven solutions.

In this introductory chapter, we will explore the foundations of AI in the kitchen, highlighting its significance, capabilities, and implications for the future of cooking and food management.

Overview of Artificial Intelligence

To embark on our journey into the AI-powered kitchen, it's essential to grasp the fundamentals of artificial intelligence. AI encompasses a broad range of technologies and techniques that enable machines to simulate human-like intelligence. From machine learning algorithms that analyze data and learn patterns to natural language processing systems that understand and generate human speech, AI is driving innovation across various domains, including the culinary realm.

Importance and Relevance of AI in the Kitchen
The kitchen is the heart of the home, where meals are prepared, memories are created, and traditions are shared. However, modern lifestyles often leave little time for elaborate meal preparation, leading to a growing demand for convenient and efficient solutions. AI has the potential to address these challenges by automating routine tasks, providing personalized recommendations, and enhancing the overall cooking experience. Moreover, with concerns about food waste, nutrition, and sustainability on the rise, AI can play a crucial role in promoting healthier and more environmentally conscious food practices.

Goals and Objectives of the Book
In this book, we aim to demystify AI in the kitchen and provide practical insights into its application and impact. Through a series of chapters covering topics such as smart kitchen appliances, meal planning algorithms, cooking assistance, and ethical considerations, we will explore the myriad ways in which AI is transforming the culinary landscape. Whether you're interested in learning about the latest smart kitchen gadgets or delving into the complexities of AI-driven recipe customization, this book offers something for everyone.

As we embark on this journey together, let us embrace the possibilities that AI brings to the kitchen, where innovation meets tradition, and technology enhances the art of cooking. Welcome to the future of food—welcome to the AI-powered kitchen.

OVERVIEW OF ARTIFICIAL INTELLIGENCE

Artificial intelligence (AI) is a branch of computer science dedicated to creating systems and machines capable of performing tasks that typically require human intelligence. These tasks include learning from experience, recognizing patterns, understanding natural language, reasoning, and problem-solving. The ultimate goal of AI is to develop machines that can mimic, augment, or even surpass human cognitive abilities.

At its core, AI is built upon the principle of using algorithms and data to enable machines to learn from their experiences, much like humans do. One of the key techniques used in AI is machine learning, which involves training algorithms on large datasets to recognize patterns and make predictions or decisions without being explicitly programmed to do so.

There are several subfields within AI, each focusing on different aspects of intelligence and problem-solving:

1. Machine Learning: Machine learning algorithms enable computers to learn from data and improve their performance over time without being explicitly programmed. This field encompasses techniques such as supervised learning, unsupervised learning, and reinforcement learning.

2. Deep Learning: Deep learning is a subset of machine learning that focuses on artificial neural networks inspired by the structure and function of the human brain. Deep learning algorithms are capable of automatically learning hierarchical representations of data, leading to breakthroughs in areas such as image and speech recognition.

3. Natural Language Processing (NLP): NLP involves teaching computers to understand, interpret, and generate human language. This field is essential for applications such as chatbots, language translation, sentiment analysis, and text summarization.

4. Computer Vision: Computer vision is concerned with enabling computers to interpret and understand visual information from the real world. This includes tasks such as object recognition, image classification, and image segmentation, with applications ranging from autonomous vehicles to medical imaging.

5. Robotics: Robotics combines AI with mechanical engineering to create intelligent machines capable of interacting with their environment. Robots equipped with AI can perform tasks such as navigation, manipulation, and collaboration in various settings, from factories to homes.

6. Recommender Systems: Recommender systems use AI algorithms to analyze user preferences and behavior and provide personalized recommendations for products, services, or content. These systems are widely used in e-commerce, streaming platforms, and social media.

7. Autonomous Agents: Autonomous agents are AI systems capable of acting independently in complex environments to achieve specific goals. Examples include self-driving cars, autonomous drones, and virtual assistants.

AI has applications across virtually every industry and domain, from healthcare and finance to entertainment and agriculture. As AI technology continues to advance, its potential to transform society and revolutionize the way we live, work, and interact with the world is virtually limitless. However, along with its promise come ethical, social, and regulatory considerations that must be carefully addressed to ensure responsible and beneficial deployment of AI systems.

IMPORTANCE AND RELEVANCE OF AI IN THE KITCHEN

The importance and relevance of AI in the kitchen stem from its potential to revolutionize how we approach cooking, meal preparation, and food management. Here are several key points highlighting why AI is becoming increasingly vital in the kitchen:

1. Efficiency and Time-Saving: In today's fast-paced world, time is a precious commodity. AI-powered kitchen appliances can automate various tasks, such as food preparation, cooking, and cleaning, allowing users to save time and effort. For busy individuals and families, this can make mealtime less stressful and more manageable.

2. Personalization and Customization: AI algorithms can analyze user preferences, dietary restrictions, and nutritional needs to provide personalized recommendations for recipes, meal plans, and grocery lists. By tailoring suggestions to individual tastes and requirements, AI helps users make healthier choices and enjoy a more satisfying culinary experience.

3. Enhanced Convenience: Smart kitchen appliances equipped with AI capabilities offer enhanced convenience and ease of use. For example, AI-enabled refrigerators can track food inventory,

suggest recipes based on available ingredients, and even place grocery orders automatically. Voice-activated assistants can provide hands-free control over cooking appliances, timers, and recipe instructions, simplifying multitasking in the kitchen.

4. Improved Food Management: AI can help users reduce food waste by monitoring expiration dates, detecting spoilage, and suggesting creative ways to use leftover ingredients. By optimizing food storage and consumption patterns, AI contributes to more sustainable and eco-friendly kitchen practices.

5. Skill Enhancement and Learning Opportunities: AI-powered cooking assistants can guide users through recipes, offering step-by-step instructions, cooking tips, and real-time feedback. Beginners can learn new culinary skills with confidence, while experienced cooks can experiment with advanced techniques and flavors with the support of AI-driven tools.

6. Innovation and Creativity: AI fosters innovation in recipe development, flavor profiling, and food pairing by analyzing vast datasets and identifying novel combinations and trends. Chefs and food enthusiasts can explore new culinary frontiers and create unique dishes with the assistance of AI-generated insights and recommendations.

7. Health and Nutrition Management: AI can play a significant role in promoting healthier eating habits and managing nutritional goals. By analyzing the nutritional content of recipes and ingredients, AI-powered apps and devices help users make informed decisions about their diet and track their intake of essential nutrients.

8. Remote Monitoring and Control: With the rise of smart home technology, AI enables users to remotely monitor and control kitchen appliances from their smartphones or other connected devices. This flexibility allows for greater convenience and peace of mind, especially for individuals with busy schedules or

mobility limitations.

Overall, the integration of AI into the kitchen represents a transformative shift in how we approach food preparation, consumption, and enjoyment. By leveraging AI technology, individuals can unlock new levels of efficiency, creativity, and satisfaction in their culinary endeavors, leading to a more enjoyable and fulfilling kitchen experience.

Goals and objectives of the book

The goals and objectives of the book "AI for Kitchen" encompass providing readers with comprehensive insights into the integration of artificial intelligence (AI) technologies into the culinary domain. Here are the overarching goals and objectives:

1. Educate Readers: The primary aim of the book is to educate readers about the potential applications and benefits of AI in the kitchen. By explaining key concepts and technologies in a clear and accessible manner, the book empowers readers to understand how AI can enhance various aspects of cooking, meal planning, and food management.

2. Explore Practical Applications: Through detailed discussions and examples, the book aims to explore the practical applications of AI in the kitchen. From smart kitchen appliances to personalized recipe recommendations and cooking assistance, readers will learn how AI-driven solutions can streamline everyday tasks and improve the overall cooking experience.

3. Provide Guidance and Insights: The book seeks to provide practical guidance and insights for individuals interested in implementing AI technologies in their own kitchens. By offering tips, best practices, and real-world examples, readers can gain a deeper understanding of how to leverage AI tools and techniques to optimize their culinary endeavors.

4. Address Challenges and Considerations: While highlighting the potential benefits of AI in the kitchen, the book also addresses challenges, ethical considerations, and potential pitfalls associated with the adoption of AI technologies. By raising awareness of these issues, readers can make informed decisions and navigate the evolving landscape of AI in a responsible and ethical manner.

5. Inspire Innovation and Exploration: By showcasing cutting-edge research, emerging trends, and innovative applications, the book aims to inspire readers to explore new possibilities and push the boundaries of AI in the kitchen. Whether readers are chefs, home cooks, food enthusiasts, or technologists, the book encourages creativity, experimentation, and innovation in culinary AI.

6. Promote Sustainability and Wellness: The book emphasizes the role of AI in promoting sustainable and healthy cooking practices. By highlighting features such as food waste reduction, nutritional analysis, and eco-friendly kitchen management, readers are encouraged to adopt more sustainable and wellness-oriented approaches to food preparation and consumption.

7. Empower Readers to Make Informed Choices: Ultimately, the goal of the book is to empower readers to make informed choices about integrating AI technologies into their kitchens. By providing a comprehensive overview of the opportunities, challenges, and considerations involved, readers can confidently embrace AI as a valuable tool for enhancing their culinary experiences.

Overall, the book "AI for Kitchen" aims to serve as a comprehensive resource for anyone interested in exploring the intersection of artificial intelligence and cooking. Whether readers are seeking practical advice, inspiration, or a deeper understanding of the potential of AI in the kitchen, the book strives to meet their needs and enrich their journey into the exciting world of culinary AI.

EVOLUTION OF TECHNOLOGY IN THE KITCHEN

The evolution of technology in the kitchen has been a fascinating journey, marked by significant advancements that have transformed the way we cook, eat, and interact with food. From rudimentary tools and appliances to sophisticated AI-driven systems, the progression of kitchen automation reflects humanity's quest for efficiency, convenience, and innovation. In this chapter, we will explore the key milestones and trends in the evolution of kitchen technology, tracing its evolution from ancient times to the modern era of AI-driven smart kitchens.

1. Early Innovations in Kitchen Technology
  - Primitive Cooking Tools: The earliest humans used basic tools such as stones, fire pits, and clay pots to prepare and cook food.
  - Invention of the Stove: The development of enclosed cooking devices, such as the hearth and stove, revolutionized cooking by providing controlled heat sources and improving cooking efficiency.
  - Introduction of Mechanical Appliances: The Industrial Revolution brought about the mass production of mechanical kitchen appliances, such as hand-cranked mixers, meat grinders, and egg beaters, which simplified food preparation tasks.

2. Emergence of Electrical Appliances

- Introduction of Electric Appliances: The early 20th century witnessed the introduction of electric appliances, including electric stoves, toasters, and refrigerators, which offered greater convenience and precision in cooking and food preservation.

- Rise of Microwave Ovens: The invention of the microwave oven in the mid-20th century revolutionized cooking by enabling rapid heating and cooking of food through microwave radiation.

3. Digital Revolution in the Kitchen

- Advent of Digital Technology: The integration of digital technology into kitchen appliances, such as programmable ovens, digital scales, and timers, enhanced precision and control in cooking processes.

- Internet Connectivity: The proliferation of internet-connected appliances and smart kitchen devices introduced new possibilities for remote monitoring, recipe sharing, and automated cooking processes.

4. Evolution of Smart Kitchen Appliances

- Rise of Smart Appliances: The advent of smart kitchen appliances equipped with sensors, actuators, and connectivity features enabled automated control, remote access, and data-driven insights for users.

- Integration of AI and Machine Learning: Recent advancements in AI and machine learning have led to the development of intelligent kitchen systems capable of learning user preferences, optimizing cooking processes, and providing personalized recommendations.

5. Trends in Kitchen Automation

- Seamless Integration: Modern kitchen automation emphasizes seamless integration and interoperability among appliances, allowing users to create cohesive smart kitchen ecosystems.

- Personalization and Customization: AI-driven kitchen technologies prioritize personalization and customization, tailoring cooking experiences, recipes, and recommendations to individual preferences and dietary requirements.

- Sustainability and Efficiency: The latest trends in kitchen automation focus on promoting sustainability and efficiency through features such as energy optimization, food waste reduction, and eco-friendly materials.

6. Future Directions

- AI-Powered Cooking Assistants: The future of kitchen automation lies in AI-powered cooking assistants capable of providing real-time guidance, recipe suggestions, and cooking tips based on user preferences and environmental conditions.

- Integration with IoT and Smart Home Systems: The convergence of kitchen automation with IoT and smart home systems will enable seamless connectivity, automation, and control of kitchen appliances and devices.

- Continued Innovation: As technology continues to advance, we can expect ongoing innovation in kitchen automation, with developments in areas such as robotics, augmented reality, and sustainable food production reshaping the future of cooking and food preparation.

In summary, the evolution of technology in the kitchen has followed a trajectory of increasing automation, connectivity, and intelligence, driven by a desire for greater efficiency, convenience, and innovation. From ancient cooking tools to AI-driven smart kitchens, the journey of kitchen automation reflects humanity's ingenuity and relentless pursuit of progress in the culinary domain. As we look ahead to the future, the possibilities for further innovation and transformation in the kitchen are boundless, promising exciting new opportunities for enhancing the way we cook, eat, and experience food.

TYPES OF KITCHEN TASKS SUITABLE FOR AUTOMATION

Automation in the kitchen involves the use of technology to streamline and simplify various culinary tasks, making cooking more efficient, convenient, and enjoyable. While not all kitchen tasks are easily automated, many lend themselves well to automation due to their repetitive nature or the need for precise control. In this section, we will explore the types of kitchen tasks that are particularly suitable for automation:

1. Food Preparation:
   - Chopping and Slicing: Automated food processors and electric slicers can quickly and precisely chop, slice, and dice ingredients, saving time and effort in meal preparation.
   - Mixing and Blending: Stand mixers, immersion blenders, and blender appliances automate the mixing, blending, and pureeing of ingredients for recipes such as sauces, soups, and smoothies.
   - Kneading Dough: Bread machines and stand mixers equipped with dough hooks automate the kneading and proofing process for bread and pastry dough, ensuring consistent results.

2. Cooking:
   - Temperature Control: Smart ovens and induction cooktops with precise temperature control features allow for automated

cooking processes, such as sous vide cooking, where maintaining a specific temperature is critical.

- Timed Cooking: Programmable slow cookers, rice cookers, and multicookers enable users to set cooking times and temperatures in advance, automating the cooking process for dishes that require long, slow cooking.

3. Food Preservation and Storage:

- Refrigeration: Smart refrigerators equipped with temperature sensors and humidity controls automate the preservation of perishable foods by maintaining optimal storage conditions and alerting users to potential issues, such as temperature fluctuations or expired items.

- Freezing: Automated ice makers and freezers regulate ice production and storage, ensuring a constant supply of ice for beverages and preserving frozen foods at the appropriate temperature.

4. Cleaning and Maintenance:

- Dishwashing: Dishwashers automate the cleaning and sanitizing of dishes, utensils, and cookware, saving time and water compared to handwashing.

- Surface Cleaning: Robotic vacuum cleaners and floor mopping robots automate the cleaning of kitchen floors and surfaces, removing dirt, crumbs, and spills with minimal supervision.

5. Inventory Management and Shopping:

- Inventory Tracking: Smart kitchen inventory systems use sensors and barcode scanning technology to track food inventory levels, expiration dates, and usage patterns, automating the process of inventory management and reducing food waste.

- Grocery Ordering: AI-powered grocery shopping apps and smart refrigerators can automate the process of generating shopping lists based on inventory levels, recipe plans, and user preferences, streamlining the grocery shopping experience.

6. Recipe Recommendations and Meal Planning:

- AI-driven Recipe Suggestions: Recipe recommendation apps and platforms leverage AI algorithms to analyze user preferences, dietary restrictions, and ingredient availability, automating the process of finding and suggesting recipes tailored to individual tastes and needs.

- Meal Planning: Meal planning apps and services use AI to generate personalized meal plans based on nutritional goals, cooking preferences, and schedule constraints, automating the process of meal planning and saving users time and effort.

By automating these types of kitchen tasks, individuals can streamline their cooking processes, save time and effort, and enjoy a more efficient and enjoyable culinary experience. As technology continues to advance, we can expect further innovations in kitchen automation, offering new opportunities to enhance convenience, creativity, and sustainability in the kitchen.

BENEFITS OF INTEGRATING AI IN KITCHEN APPLIANCES

The integration of artificial intelligence (AI) into kitchen appliances offers a multitude of benefits, revolutionizing the way we cook, eat, and interact with food. By leveraging AI technologies, kitchen appliances can become smarter, more intuitive, and more efficient, enhancing the overall culinary experience for users. Here are some of the key benefits of integrating AI in kitchen appliances:

1. Enhanced Efficiency: AI-powered kitchen appliances can streamline cooking processes, automate routine tasks, and optimize resource usage, leading to increased efficiency in the kitchen. By leveraging algorithms to anticipate user needs, adjust settings dynamically, and optimize cooking times, AI helps users save time and effort in meal preparation.

2. Personalized Recommendations: AI algorithms can analyze user preferences, dietary restrictions, and ingredient availability to provide personalized recipe recommendations, cooking suggestions, and meal plans. By tailoring recommendations to individual tastes and needs, AI-powered appliances empower users to discover new recipes, explore diverse cuisines, and make informed choices about their meals.

3. Improved Accuracy and Precision: AI enables kitchen appliances to achieve greater accuracy and precision in cooking

processes, temperature control, and ingredient measurements. Whether it's sous vide cooking with precise temperature regulation or baking with exact ingredient proportions, AI ensures consistent and reliable results, enhancing the quality of cooked food.

4. Smart Monitoring and Control: AI-equipped kitchen appliances can monitor cooking progress, detect anomalies, and adjust settings automatically to optimize performance and ensure optimal outcomes. For example, smart ovens can adjust cooking temperatures and times based on real-time feedback, while smart refrigerators can alert users to food spoilage or expiration dates.

5. Convenient Voice and Gesture Control: Integration with voice recognition and gesture control technologies allows users to interact with AI-powered kitchen appliances using natural language commands or intuitive gestures. This hands-free control capability enhances convenience and accessibility, especially for users with mobility limitations or busy lifestyles.

6. Energy Efficiency and Resource Conservation: AI algorithms can optimize energy usage, reduce resource wastage, and minimize environmental impact in the kitchen. By optimizing cooking processes, managing appliance usage, and promoting sustainable food practices, AI-powered appliances contribute to energy efficiency and resource conservation, aligning with eco-friendly principles.

7. Continuous Learning and Improvement: AI systems can learn from user interactions, feedback, and data insights to continuously improve their performance and adapt to changing preferences and conditions. By leveraging machine learning algorithms, kitchen appliances can become smarter over time, offering increasingly personalized and efficient cooking experiences for users.

8. Seamless Integration with Smart Home Ecosystems: AI-

powered kitchen appliances can seamlessly integrate with other smart home devices and platforms, creating a cohesive smart home ecosystem centered around the kitchen. Whether it's syncing with smart lighting systems, home security cameras, or voice assistants, AI-enabled appliances enhance connectivity and interoperability, enabling users to control and manage their kitchen environment more effectively.

Overall, the integration of AI in kitchen appliances offers a range of benefits that enhance convenience, efficiency, and culinary creativity. By harnessing the power of AI technologies, kitchen appliances can become indispensable tools that empower users to cook with confidence, explore new flavors, and enjoy a more personalized and enjoyable cooking experience.

SMART REFRIGERATORS

Smart refrigerators represent a significant advancement in kitchen technology, offering a range of features and capabilities that go beyond simple food storage. Here's a closer look at smart refrigerators and their role in food management:

1. Inventory Management:
   - Automatic Inventory Tracking: Smart refrigerators use built-in cameras, sensors, and barcode scanners to automatically track the contents of the refrigerator. This includes monitoring items such as fruits, vegetables, dairy products, and beverages.
   - Expiration Date Tracking: By recognizing expiration dates on food items, smart refrigerators can alert users when items are nearing their expiry and suggest using them before they spoil.
   - Inventory Logging: Users can conveniently view the inventory of their refrigerator remotely through smartphone apps or the refrigerator's built-in display, allowing them to check what items they have on hand while grocery shopping or meal planning.

2. Food Management and Organization:
   - Customizable Storage Zones: Smart refrigerators often feature customizable storage zones with adjustable shelves and compartments, allowing users to organize food items based on their preferences and storage needs.

- Temperature and Humidity Control: Some smart refrigerators offer precise temperature and humidity controls for different compartments, such as crisper drawers for fruits and vegetables, to extend the shelf life of perishable items and maintain optimal freshness.

- Recipe Suggestions and Meal Planning: Smart refrigerators can suggest recipes based on the ingredients stored inside, helping users make use of items before they expire and inspiring meal ideas based on available ingredients.

3. Connectivity and Integration:

- Smartphone Integration: Users can monitor and control their smart refrigerators remotely using smartphone apps. This allows for tasks such as adjusting temperature settings, checking inventory, and receiving notifications about maintenance or issues.

- Integration with Virtual Assistants: Smart refrigerators often integrate with virtual assistants like Amazon Alexa or Google Assistant, enabling hands-free voice commands for tasks such as adding items to shopping lists, checking the weather, or playing music.

- Compatibility with Smart Home Systems: Smart refrigerators can be part of a larger smart home ecosystem, integrating with other connected devices such as smart lighting, thermostats, and security systems for enhanced convenience and automation.

4. Energy Efficiency and Sustainability:

- Energy-Saving Features: Smart refrigerators often come equipped with energy-saving features such as LED lighting, temperature sensors, and advanced insulation materials to reduce energy consumption and lower utility bills.

- Food Waste Reduction: By helping users keep track of their food inventory, expiration dates, and usage patterns, smart refrigerators contribute to reducing food waste and promoting more sustainable food management practices.

5. Data Insights and Analytics:

- Usage Data Analysis: Smart refrigerators can collect data on usage patterns, temperature settings, and energy consumption, providing users with insights into their food storage habits and appliance performance.

- Recommendations and Insights: Based on usage data and analytics, smart refrigerators can offer personalized recommendations and insights to help users optimize their food management practices and improve efficiency.

In summary, smart refrigerators play a crucial role in food management by offering advanced features such as automatic inventory tracking, customizable storage options, connectivity with smartphones and virtual assistants, energy-efficient operation, and data-driven insights. By leveraging these capabilities, users can enjoy greater convenience, efficiency, and sustainability in their kitchen routines.

AI-ENABLED COOKING APPLIANCES

AI-enabled cooking appliances, including ovens, stoves, and other kitchen gadgets, are transforming the culinary landscape by offering innovative features and capabilities that enhance convenience, precision, and creativity in cooking. Here's an overview of AI-enabled cooking appliances and their benefits:

1. Precision Cooking:

- Temperature Control: AI-enabled ovens and stoves feature precise temperature control capabilities, allowing users to cook dishes at optimal temperatures for perfect results every time. AI algorithms can adjust temperature settings dynamically based on the type of food being cooked and desired doneness.

- Cooking Profiles: These appliances often come with pre-programmed cooking profiles for various dishes, such as roasts, baked goods, and vegetables. Users can select the desired cooking profile, and the appliance will automatically adjust settings to achieve the best results.

2. Recipe Recommendations and Guidance:

- AI-Powered Recipe Suggestions: Some AI-enabled cooking appliances offer recipe suggestions based on user preferences, dietary restrictions, and ingredient availability. These appliances can analyze user data and recommend recipes that suit their tastes and cooking style.

- Step-by-Step Guidance: AI algorithms can provide step-by-step cooking guidance, offering instructions on when to add ingredients, adjust settings, and perform cooking techniques. This feature is particularly useful for novice cooks or individuals trying out new recipes.

3. Adaptive Cooking Algorithms:

- Learning Capabilities: AI-enabled cooking appliances can learn from user interactions and feedback to improve cooking performance over time. By analyzing data on cooking outcomes and user preferences, these appliances can adapt their cooking algorithms to deliver better results with each use.

- Personalized Settings: Some appliances allow users to create personalized cooking profiles that store their preferred settings and cooking preferences. This enables a customized cooking experience tailored to individual tastes and requirements.

4. Remote Monitoring and Control:

- Smartphone Connectivity: Many AI-enabled cooking appliances can be controlled remotely via smartphone apps, allowing users to monitor cooking progress, adjust settings, and receive notifications from anywhere. This feature offers flexibility and convenience, especially for busy individuals or those with unpredictable schedules.

- Voice Control Integration: Integration with virtual assistants like Amazon Alexa or Google Assistant enables hands-free voice commands for controlling AI-enabled cooking appliances. Users can simply use voice commands to preheat the oven, set timers, or adjust cooking settings.

5. Energy Efficiency and Safety:

- Energy-Saving Features: AI-enabled cooking appliances often come equipped with energy-saving features such as programmable timers, automatic shut-off, and energy-efficient cooking modes. These features help reduce energy consumption and lower utility bills.

- Safety Sensors: Advanced safety features, such as

temperature sensors and smoke detectors, ensure safe operation and prevent accidents such as overcooking or burning food. AI algorithms can analyze sensor data and take corrective actions to mitigate potential risks.

6. Integration with Smart Home Ecosystems:

- Seamless Integration: AI-enabled cooking appliances can seamlessly integrate with other smart home devices and platforms, creating a cohesive smart kitchen ecosystem. Users can synchronize their appliances with smart lighting, thermostats, and security systems for enhanced convenience and automation.

- Data Sharing and Insights: Integration with smart home ecosystems allows for data sharing and insights across different devices, enabling users to optimize energy usage, track usage patterns, and receive personalized recommendations for improving efficiency and performance.

In summary, AI-enabled cooking appliances offer a range of benefits, including precision cooking, recipe recommendations, remote monitoring and control, energy efficiency, safety features, and integration with smart home ecosystems. By leveraging AI technology, these appliances empower users to cook with confidence, creativity, and convenience, revolutionizing the way we approach cooking and meal preparation.

AUTOMATED KITCHEN CLEANING DEVICES

Automated kitchen cleaning devices represent a significant advancement in household technology, offering convenience, efficiency, and time savings in maintaining a clean and hygienic kitchen environment. Here's an overview of automated kitchen cleaning devices and their benefits:

1. Robotic Vacuum Cleaners:
   - Efficient Floor Cleaning: Robotic vacuum cleaners are designed to autonomously navigate and clean kitchen floors, removing dirt, dust, and debris. Equipped with sensors and mapping technology, these devices can detect obstacles, avoid collisions, and navigate around furniture and kitchen appliances.
   - Scheduled Cleaning: Users can schedule cleaning sessions in advance, allowing the robotic vacuum cleaner to automatically clean the kitchen at specified times, such as when the house is empty or during off-peak hours.
   - Hands-Free Operation: Robotic vacuum cleaners offer hands-free operation, requiring minimal supervision or manual intervention. Users can simply set up the device, activate cleaning modes, and let it do the work while they attend to other tasks.

2. Robotic Mops and Floor Scrubbers:
   - Mopping and Scrubbing: Robotic mops and floor scrubbers are designed to automate the process of mopping and scrubbing kitchen floors, removing stains, spills, and dried-on

residue. These devices use advanced cleaning techniques, such as vibrating brushes and water sprayers, to achieve thorough cleaning results.

- Multi-Surface Cleaning: Robotic mops and floor scrubbers are suitable for various types of kitchen flooring, including tile, hardwood, laminate, and vinyl. They can adapt to different surface textures and adjust cleaning intensity accordingly.

- Efficient Water Management: Some robotic mops and floor scrubbers feature intelligent water management systems that control water usage and prevent over-saturation of floors. This helps minimize water waste and reduce drying time after cleaning.

3. Automated Dishwashers:
- Efficient Dish Cleaning: Automated dishwashers offer a convenient and efficient way to clean dishes, utensils, and cookware in the kitchen. Equipped with powerful jets, spray arms, and detergent dispensers, dishwashers can remove food residues and grease effectively, leaving dishes sparkling clean.

- Programmable Cleaning Cycles: Dishwashers feature multiple cleaning cycles, such as normal, heavy-duty, eco-friendly, and quick wash, allowing users to select the most suitable cycle based on the level of soiling and the type of dishes being washed.

- Energy and Water Efficiency: Modern dishwashers are designed to be energy and water-efficient, incorporating features such as eco-friendly wash cycles, soil sensors, and water-saving options. This helps reduce utility bills and minimize environmental impact.

4. Self-Cleaning Ovens:
- Automatic Cleaning Cycles: Self-cleaning ovens feature automatic cleaning cycles that use high temperatures to burn off food residues and grease, reducing them to ash. After the cleaning cycle is complete, users can simply wipe away the ash with a damp cloth, leaving the oven clean and ready for use.

- Time-Saving Convenience: Self-cleaning ovens offer a convenient alternative to manual oven cleaning, which can be time-consuming and labor-intensive. Users can initiate the cleaning cycle with the push of a button and continue with other tasks while the oven cleans itself.

- Safety Features: Self-cleaning ovens are equipped with safety features to prevent accidents and ensure user protection during the cleaning process. These features may include automatic door locking mechanisms, insulation to prevent heat transfer to the exterior, and temperature sensors to monitor internal oven temperatures.

5. Automated Trash Cans:

- Hands-Free Operation: Automated trash cans feature motion sensors or touchless controls that allow users to open the lid without touching the can, minimizing the spread of germs and bacteria. This hands-free operation is convenient when disposing of food scraps and waste during cooking or meal preparation.

- Odor Control: Some automated trash cans come equipped with odor control features, such as built-in carbon filters or deodorizer compartments, that help neutralize unpleasant odors and keep the kitchen smelling fresh.

- Convenient Waste Management: Automated trash cans streamline waste management in the kitchen by offering features such as bag liners, bag holders, and bag dispensers that simplify the process of replacing trash bags and disposing of waste.

6. Smart Cleaning Devices:

- Integration with Smart Home Ecosystems: Many automated kitchen cleaning devices can integrate with smart home ecosystems, allowing users to control and monitor them remotely using smartphone apps or voice commands. This integration enables features such as scheduling cleaning sessions, receiving notifications, and accessing usage data and insights.

- Data Insights and Analytics: Smart cleaning devices can collect data on cleaning performance, usage patterns, and maintenance needs, providing users with insights and recommendations for optimizing cleaning routines and appliance performance.

- Energy Efficiency and Sustainability: Automated cleaning devices are designed to be energy-efficient and environmentally friendly, incorporating features such as energy-saving modes, eco-friendly cleaning solutions, and recyclable materials. This helps reduce energy consumption, minimize environmental impact, and promote sustainability in the kitchen.

In summary, automated kitchen cleaning devices offer a range of benefits, including efficient floor cleaning, hands-free operation, programmable cleaning cycles, energy and water efficiency, and integration with smart home ecosystems. By automating cleaning tasks in the kitchen, these devices help users save time and effort, maintain a clean and hygienic environment, and enjoy greater convenience and peace of mind in their daily lives.

INTEGRATION WITH VOICE ASSISTANTS

Integration with voice assistants like Amazon Alexa or Google Assistant adds an extra layer of convenience and functionality to smart kitchen appliances. Here's how integration with voice assistants enhances the capabilities of smart kitchen appliances:

1. Hands-Free Control:
   - Users can control their smart kitchen appliances using voice commands, eliminating the need for manual interaction with buttons or touchscreens. This hands-free control is especially convenient when users have their hands occupied with cooking tasks or when they're in another room and unable to physically access the appliance.

2. Seamless Interaction:
   - Voice assistants provide a natural and intuitive interface for interacting with smart kitchen appliances. Users can simply speak commands or ask questions in natural language, making it easy to operate appliances even for those who are not tech-savvy.

3. Multi-Appliance Control:
   - Voice assistants allow users to control multiple smart kitchen appliances simultaneously or in sequence with a single voice command. For example, users can ask the voice assistant to preheat the oven, set a timer, and turn on the coffee maker all at once, streamlining cooking routines and enhancing efficiency.

4. Remote Control:
- Integration with voice assistants enables remote control of smart kitchen appliances via smartphone apps or voice commands issued from anywhere with an internet connection. This allows users to monitor and control their appliances even when they're away from home, providing greater flexibility and convenience.

5. Customizable Commands:
- Users can customize voice commands to suit their preferences and routines, enabling personalized interactions with smart kitchen appliances. For example, users can create custom commands like "Alexa, start baking mode" or "Hey Google, brew coffee at 7 a.m." to initiate specific actions or routines tailored to their needs.

6. Smart Home Integration:
- Voice assistants facilitate seamless integration with other smart home devices and systems, allowing users to create interconnected ecosystems of smart appliances, lighting, thermostats, and security systems. This integration enables advanced automation and coordination of various home functions, enhancing convenience and efficiency.

7. Accessibility Features:
- Voice assistants enhance accessibility for users with disabilities or mobility limitations by providing alternative control options that do not require physical interaction with appliances. This inclusivity ensures that everyone can benefit from the convenience and functionality of smart kitchen appliances.

8. Enhanced Capabilities:
- Integration with voice assistants enables smart kitchen appliances to perform additional functions beyond their built-in capabilities. For example, users can ask for recipe recommendations, cooking tips, or nutritional information, or

they can request to receive alerts and notifications from their appliances.

In summary, integration with voice assistants like Amazon Alexa or Google Assistant enhances the usability, convenience, and functionality of smart kitchen appliances by providing hands-free control, seamless interaction, multi-appliance control, remote access, customizable commands, smart home integration, accessibility features, and enhanced capabilities. By leveraging voice assistants, users can simplify their cooking routines, streamline kitchen tasks, and enjoy greater convenience and control over their smart kitchen appliances.

MEAL PLANNING ALGORITHMS

AI-powered meal planning algorithms and applications leverage machine learning, data analytics, and user preferences to offer personalized meal plans, recipe suggestions, and grocery lists tailored to individual tastes, dietary needs, and lifestyle preferences. Here's how these algorithms and applications work:

1. Data Collection and Analysis:

   - Meal planning algorithms gather data from various sources, including user input, recipe databases, nutritional databases, and food inventory information. This data is analyzed to identify patterns, preferences, and dietary requirements.

2. User Preferences and Goals:

   - Users provide input regarding their dietary preferences, culinary preferences, cooking skills, health goals, and lifestyle factors such as budget and time constraints. This information is used to customize meal plans and recipe suggestions.

3. Recipe Recommendation Engine:

   - Using machine learning algorithms, the meal planning application generates recipe recommendations based on user preferences and available ingredients. These recommendations may take into account factors such as flavor profiles, cooking techniques, nutritional content, and ingredient availability.

4. Nutritional Analysis:

   - Meal planning algorithms analyze the nutritional content of recipes to ensure they align with users' dietary goals and nutritional needs. This includes tracking calories, macronutrients (such as protein, carbohydrates, and fats), vitamins, minerals, and other dietary components.

5. Meal Plan Generation:

- Based on user preferences, dietary goals, and nutritional requirements, the meal planning application generates personalized meal plans for various time periods, such as weekly or monthly plans. These meal plans include breakfast, lunch, dinner, and snacks, with options for customization and flexibility.

6. Grocery List Generation:

- The meal planning application automatically generates a grocery list based on the ingredients required for the selected recipes in the meal plan. Users can review and edit the grocery list as needed, adding or removing items and adjusting quantities.

7. Adaptive Learning:

- Meal planning algorithms continuously learn from user feedback and behavior to improve the accuracy and relevance of recipe recommendations and meal plans over time. As users interact with the application and provide feedback on recipes, the algorithm adjusts its recommendations to better suit their preferences and needs.

8. Integration with Smart Kitchen Appliances:

- Some meal planning applications integrate with smart kitchen appliances to streamline the cooking process further. Users can synchronize their meal plans with smart ovens, multicookers, and other appliances, allowing for seamless execution of recipes and cooking instructions.

9. Mobile Apps and Web Platforms:

- Meal planning applications are accessible via mobile apps and web platforms, allowing users to access their meal plans, recipes, and grocery lists from anywhere with an internet connection. Users can also receive notifications, reminders, and updates related to their meal plans.

10. Social and Community Features:

   - Some meal planning applications incorporate social and community features, allowing users to share recipes, meal plans, and cooking tips with others. This fosters a sense of community and encourages collaboration and engagement among users with similar interests and goals.

In summary, AI-powered meal planning algorithms and applications offer personalized meal plans, recipe suggestions, and grocery lists tailored to individual preferences and dietary needs. By leveraging machine learning and data analytics, these applications simplify the meal planning process, save time and effort, and help users make informed choices about their nutrition and cooking routines.

PERSONALIZED RECIPE SUGGESTIONS

Personalized recipe suggestions based on dietary preferences and restrictions are a key feature of many AI-powered meal planning and recipe recommendation platforms. These platforms use machine learning algorithms to analyze user input, dietary requirements, and culinary preferences to generate tailored recipe suggestions. Here's how personalized recipe suggestions based on dietary preferences and restrictions work:

1. User Input:
   - Users provide input regarding their dietary preferences, such as vegetarian, vegan, gluten-free, dairy-free, paleo, keto, or specific food allergies or intolerances. They may also specify preferences for certain cuisines, ingredients, cooking techniques, or meal types.

2. Dietary Restrictions and Requirements:
   - Based on the user's input, the recipe recommendation platform identifies dietary restrictions and requirements that need to be considered when generating recipe suggestions. This may include avoiding certain ingredients, such as dairy, nuts, soy, or gluten, or adhering to specific dietary guidelines, such as low-carb or high-protein diets.

3. Recipe Database:
   - The platform maintains a database of recipes curated from various sources, including professional chefs, food bloggers,

culinary experts, and user submissions. Each recipe is tagged with metadata, such as ingredients, dietary labels, cooking methods, and nutritional information.

4. Machine Learning Algorithms:
- Using machine learning algorithms, the recipe recommendation platform analyzes user preferences and dietary restrictions to identify patterns and correlations in recipe data. This enables the platform to generate personalized recipe suggestions that align with the user's dietary preferences and restrictions.

5. Content Filtering and Ranking:
- The platform applies content filtering and ranking algorithms to prioritize recipe suggestions that meet the user's dietary preferences and restrictions. Recipes that contain prohibited ingredients or do not align with the user's dietary requirements are filtered out or ranked lower in the recommendation list.

6. Nutritional Analysis:
- Recipe recommendation platforms perform nutritional analysis on recommended recipes to ensure they meet the user's dietary goals and nutritional needs. This includes tracking macronutrients (such as protein, carbohydrates, and fats), micronutrients (such as vitamins and minerals), and calorie content.

7. Personalized Recommendations:
- Based on the user's dietary preferences, restrictions, and nutritional goals, the recipe recommendation platform generates personalized recipe suggestions tailored to their individual needs. These recommendations may include breakfast, lunch, dinner, snacks, and dessert options, with options for customization and flexibility.

8. Continuous Learning and Improvement:
- Recipe recommendation platforms continuously learn from

user interactions and feedback to improve the accuracy and relevance of recipe suggestions over time. As users rate recipes, save favorites, or provide feedback on suggested recipes, the platform adjusts its recommendations to better suit their preferences and needs.

9. Integration with Meal Planning:

- Some recipe recommendation platforms integrate with meal planning applications to streamline the process of incorporating recommended recipes into weekly meal plans. Users can easily add recommended recipes to their meal plans and generate corresponding grocery lists based on the ingredients required.

In summary, personalized recipe suggestions based on dietary preferences and restrictions leverage machine learning algorithms to analyze user input, identify dietary requirements, and generate tailored recipe recommendations. By offering personalized and relevant recipe suggestions, these platforms help users make informed choices about their nutrition, simplify meal planning, and discover new culinary experiences that align with their dietary goals and preferences.

GROCERY LIST GENERATION AND INTEGRATION

Grocery list generation and integration with online shopping platforms is a valuable feature offered by many meal planning and recipe recommendation applications. Here's how it works:

1. Recipe Ingredient Analysis:
   - When users select recipes from the platform, the application analyzes the ingredients required for each recipe.

2. Ingredient Aggregation:
   - The application aggregates the ingredients from all selected recipes into a single comprehensive grocery list. This ensures that users have a complete list of all the items they need to prepare the chosen recipes.

3. Quantity Adjustment:
   - The application may also adjust the quantities of ingredients based on the number of servings users intend to prepare. This ensures that the grocery list reflects the appropriate amounts needed for the desired number of servings.

4. Categorization and Organization:
   - The grocery list is organized into categories such as produce, dairy, meat, pantry staples, and spices to make shopping more efficient. This categorization helps users navigate the grocery store and locate items more easily.

5. Integration with Online Shopping Platforms:
   - Many meal planning and recipe recommendation applications integrate with popular online shopping platforms such as Amazon Fresh, Instacart, or Walmart Grocery. Users can transfer their grocery lists directly to these platforms with a few clicks.

6. Seamless Ordering Process:
   - Once the grocery list is transferred to the online shopping platform, users can review and edit the list as needed before placing their order. The integration streamlines the ordering process, saving time and effort compared to manually inputting each item into the shopping cart.

7. Real-Time Inventory Management:
   - Some applications offer real-time inventory management features that allow users to track their pantry stock and mark items as purchased. This ensures that users only purchase items they need and helps prevent overstocking or duplicate purchases.

8. Price Comparison and Deals:
   - Integration with online shopping platforms may also include features for price comparison and deals. Users can compare prices for items across different retailers and take advantage of discounts, promotions, and coupons to save money on their grocery purchases.

9. Synchronization Across Devices:
   - Grocery lists generated by the application can be synchronized across multiple devices, allowing users to access and edit their lists from smartphones, tablets, or computers. This ensures that users always have their up-to-date grocery list on hand while shopping.

10. Smart Home Integration:
   - Some applications integrate with smart home devices such

as voice assistants or smart refrigerators. Users can add items to their grocery lists using voice commands or by scanning barcodes with a smart refrigerator's built-in camera.

In summary, grocery list generation and integration with online shopping platforms streamline the meal planning and grocery shopping process, saving time and effort for users. By automatically aggregating ingredients from selected recipes into a comprehensive grocery list and integrating with online shopping platforms, these applications offer a convenient and efficient way for users to plan meals, shop for groceries, and manage their pantry stock.

AI-BASED FOOD SPOILAGE DETECTION

AI-based food spoilage detection systems utilize advanced algorithms and sensor technology to monitor food quality and safety, detecting signs of spoilage or contamination in perishable food items. Here's how these systems work:

1. Sensor Integration:
   - AI-based food spoilage detection systems are equipped with various sensors capable of monitoring different parameters such as temperature, humidity, gases (e.g., ethylene), pH levels, and microbial activity. These sensors are strategically placed within refrigerators, storage areas, or packaging to capture data on food conditions.

2. Data Collection:
   - The sensors continuously collect data on the environmental conditions surrounding the food items, as well as any changes in these conditions over time. This data is then transmitted to a central processing unit or cloud-based server for analysis.

3. Machine Learning Algorithms:
   - Machine learning algorithms, including deep learning models, are trained using large datasets of food quality and safety indicators. These algorithms learn to identify patterns and correlations between sensor data and the presence of spoilage or contamination in food items.

4. Spoilage Detection:
   - The AI-based system analyzes the sensor data in real-time

to detect anomalies or deviations from normal conditions that may indicate food spoilage or contamination. For example, an increase in temperature beyond a certain threshold or a sudden rise in ethylene gas levels could signal the onset of spoilage.

5. Image Recognition:
  - In addition to sensor data, some AI-based systems incorporate image recognition technology to visually assess the appearance of food items. By analyzing images of food samples, the system can detect visual cues associated with spoilage, such as discoloration, mold growth, or texture changes.

6. Threshold Alerts:
  - When the AI-based system detects potential signs of spoilage or contamination, it generates alerts or notifications to notify users or food service professionals. These alerts may be sent via email, text message, or mobile app, providing timely warnings to take corrective action.

7. Adaptive Learning:
  - Over time, the AI-based system continues to learn and improve its detection capabilities based on feedback from users and new data inputs. It adapts its algorithms to become more accurate in identifying spoilage indicators specific to different types of food items and storage conditions.

8. Integration with Food Supply Chain:
  - AI-based food spoilage detection systems can be integrated into the food supply chain to monitor food quality and safety at various stages, from production and processing to distribution and retail. By identifying potential spoilage issues early on, these systems help minimize food waste and ensure consumer safety.

9. Remote Monitoring and Control:
  - Some AI-based systems offer remote monitoring and control capabilities, allowing users to access real-time data and receive alerts from anywhere with an internet connection. This enables

proactive management of food quality and safety, even when users are not physically present.

10. Compliance and Regulatory Standards:

- AI-based food spoilage detection systems help businesses and food service providers comply with food safety regulations and standards by ensuring that perishable food items are stored and handled under appropriate conditions. This reduces the risk of foodborne illness outbreaks and liability issues.

In summary, AI-based food spoilage detection systems leverage sensor technology, machine learning algorithms, and image recognition to monitor food quality and safety, detect signs of spoilage or contamination, and provide timely alerts to users. By enabling proactive management of food quality and safety, these systems help reduce food waste, ensure consumer satisfaction, and enhance overall food safety in various settings, including households, restaurants, supermarkets, and food processing facilities.

SMART FOOD STORAGE SOLUTIONS

Smart food storage solutions utilize advanced technology to monitor, track, and maintain the quality and safety of stored food items. These solutions employ various sensors, connectivity options, and automation features to optimize food storage conditions and reduce the risk of spoilage or contamination. Here's an overview of smart food storage solutions:

1. Temperature and Humidity Monitoring:
   - Smart food storage solutions are equipped with sensors that monitor temperature and humidity levels inside refrigerators, freezers, and pantry cabinets. These sensors ensure that food items are stored at optimal conditions to prevent spoilage and maintain freshness.

2. Real-time Monitoring and Alerts:
   - The sensors in smart food storage solutions provide real-time data on temperature and humidity levels, allowing users to monitor conditions remotely via smartphone apps or web interfaces. In case of any deviations from the optimal range, the system sends alerts or notifications to users, prompting them to take corrective action.

3. Inventory Management:
   - Smart food storage solutions help users keep track of their food inventory by automatically logging the items stored inside. Some systems use barcode scanning or image recognition

technology to identify and catalog food items, while others rely on manual input from users. This inventory management feature helps users avoid food waste by ensuring that items are used before they expire.

4. Expiration Date Tracking:

- Smart food storage solutions can track the expiration dates of perishable food items and send reminders to users when items are nearing their expiration. This helps users consume food items before they spoil and reduce the risk of foodborne illness.

5. Air Quality Monitoring:

- Some advanced smart food storage solutions include sensors that monitor air quality inside refrigerators and storage containers. These sensors detect gases such as ethylene, which can accelerate the ripening and spoilage of fruits and vegetables. By maintaining optimal air quality, these systems help extend the shelf life of perishable food items.

6. Adaptive Cooling and Preservation:

- Smart refrigerators and storage containers may feature adaptive cooling technology that adjusts temperature settings based on the type of food being stored and its optimal storage conditions. This helps preserve the freshness and quality of food items while minimizing energy consumption.

7. Integration with Meal Planning:

- Smart food storage solutions can integrate with meal planning and recipe recommendation applications to streamline the meal preparation process. Users can access their inventory of stored food items and receive recipe suggestions based on available ingredients, making meal planning more convenient and efficient.

8. Voice Control and Smart Home Integration:

- Many smart food storage solutions offer voice control capabilities, allowing users to interact with the system using voice commands via virtual assistants like Amazon Alexa or Google Assistant. Additionally, these solutions may integrate with other smart home devices and platforms, enabling seamless automation and coordination of various home functions.

9. Energy Efficiency and Sustainability:

- Smart food storage solutions are designed to be energy-efficient, incorporating features such as LED lighting, insulation, and energy-saving modes to minimize energy consumption. By reducing energy usage, these systems help lower utility bills and promote sustainability.

10. Data Insights and Analytics:

- Smart food storage solutions collect data on food usage patterns, storage conditions, and user preferences, providing valuable insights to users. These insights can help users optimize their food storage practices, reduce food waste, and make informed decisions about purchasing and meal planning.

In summary, smart food storage solutions offer a range of features and capabilities to monitor, track, and maintain the quality and safety of stored food items. By leveraging advanced technology and automation, these solutions help users optimize their food storage practices, reduce food waste, and ensure that food items remain fresh and safe for consumption.

MONITORING KITCHEN HYGIENE AND SAFETY

Monitoring kitchen hygiene and safety with AI sensors involves utilizing advanced sensor technology and artificial intelligence to detect potential hazards, ensure proper hygiene practices, and maintain a safe environment in the kitchen. Here's how it works:

1. Sensor Integration:
   - AI sensors are strategically placed in various areas of the kitchen to monitor environmental conditions, detect contaminants, and track hygiene practices. These sensors may include cameras, temperature sensors, motion sensors, humidity sensors, and gas sensors.

2. Contaminant Detection:
   - AI sensors analyze data in real-time to detect potential contaminants in the kitchen environment, such as bacteria, pathogens, or chemical residues. For example, sensors may detect the presence of harmful bacteria on food preparation surfaces or in food storage areas.

3. Hygiene Monitoring:
   - AI sensors monitor hygiene practices in the kitchen, such as handwashing compliance, surface cleaning frequency, and food handling procedures. Sensors may detect motion patterns or monitor activity levels to ensure that proper hygiene protocols are followed.

4. Temperature Monitoring:

- Temperature sensors are used to monitor food storage temperatures, ensuring that perishable food items are stored at safe temperatures to prevent spoilage and bacterial growth. Sensors may also detect temperature fluctuations in cooking appliances to ensure that food is cooked to the appropriate temperature to kill harmful bacteria.

5. Hazard Detection:

- AI sensors identify potential hazards in the kitchen, such as spills, leaks, or malfunctioning appliances. Sensors may detect anomalies in the environment, such as smoke, gas leaks, or unusual odors, and generate alerts to notify users of potential safety risks.

6. Real-time Alerts and Notifications:

- When AI sensors detect potential hygiene or safety issues in the kitchen, they generate real-time alerts and notifications to notify users or kitchen staff. Alerts may be sent via smartphone apps, email, or text messages, prompting users to take immediate action to address the issue.

7. Predictive Analytics:

- AI sensors analyze historical data and usage patterns to predict potential hygiene or safety risks in the kitchen. By identifying trends and patterns, sensors can anticipate potential issues before they occur and provide proactive recommendations for mitigating risks.

8. Integration with Smart Kitchen Appliances:

- AI sensors integrate with smart kitchen appliances to enhance safety and hygiene in the kitchen. For example, sensors may detect when a stove is left unattended or when a refrigerator door is left open, prompting automatic shut-off or alerts to prevent accidents or food spoilage.

9. Compliance Monitoring:

- AI sensors help ensure compliance with food safety regulations and standards by monitoring hygiene practices and environmental conditions in the kitchen. Sensors may provide documentation and audit trails to demonstrate compliance with regulatory requirements.

10. Data Insights and Analysis:

- AI sensors collect data on kitchen hygiene and safety practices, providing valuable insights and analytics to users. Data analysis can identify areas for improvement, track performance metrics, and inform decision-making to optimize kitchen hygiene and safety protocols.

In summary, monitoring kitchen hygiene and safety with AI sensors involves leveraging advanced sensor technology and artificial intelligence to detect contaminants, ensure proper hygiene practices, and maintain a safe environment in the kitchen. By providing real-time alerts, predictive analytics, and data insights, AI sensors help users optimize kitchen hygiene and safety protocols to prevent foodborne illness and ensure a healthy and safe cooking environment.

AI-DRIVEN RECIPE MODIFICATION FOR HEALTH

AI-driven recipe modification for health or taste preferences involves utilizing machine learning algorithms to analyze existing recipes and make adjustments based on user preferences, dietary restrictions, or nutritional goals. Here's how it works:

1. Recipe Analysis:
   - The AI system analyzes existing recipes, including ingredients, cooking methods, and nutritional information, to understand their composition and flavor profiles.

2. User Input:
   - Users provide input regarding their health goals, taste preferences, dietary restrictions, and ingredient preferences. This input helps the AI system understand the specific modifications needed to align the recipe with the user's preferences.

3. Machine Learning Algorithms:
   - Machine learning algorithms process the recipe data and user input to generate personalized recommendations for modifying the recipe. These algorithms learn from user feedback and behavior to improve the accuracy and relevance of their recommendations over time.

4. Health Modifications:

- For users with specific health goals, such as weight loss, heart health, or managing dietary conditions like diabetes or hypertension, the AI system may recommend modifications to reduce calorie content, saturated fat, sodium, or sugar levels in the recipe. This could involve substituting ingredients, adjusting portion sizes, or modifying cooking methods to make the recipe healthier.

5. Taste Enhancements:

- For users seeking to enhance the flavor and enjoyment of the recipe, the AI system may recommend modifications to enhance taste, texture, or visual appeal. This could involve adding herbs, spices, or seasonings to enhance flavor, incorporating cooking techniques to improve texture, or garnishing with colorful ingredients to enhance visual presentation.

6. Ingredient Substitutions:

- The AI system may recommend ingredient substitutions to accommodate dietary restrictions or preferences. For example, it may suggest dairy-free alternatives for users with lactose intolerance, gluten-free alternatives for users with celiac disease, or plant-based alternatives for users following a vegetarian or vegan diet.

7. Nutritional Analysis:

- After making modifications to the recipe, the AI system performs a nutritional analysis to ensure that the modified recipe aligns with the user's nutritional goals and dietary requirements. This analysis includes calculating calorie counts, macronutrient composition (protein, carbohydrates, fats), and micronutrient content (vitamins, minerals).

8. Personalized Recommendations:

- The AI system generates personalized recommendations for modifying the recipe based on the user's preferences and goals. These recommendations may include specific ingredient substitutions, cooking techniques, or portion adjustments tailored to the user's individual needs.

9. Recipe Testing and Feedback:
- Users have the opportunity to test the modified recipe and provide feedback on the taste, texture, and overall satisfaction. This feedback helps the AI system learn and refine its recommendations for future recipe modifications, ensuring ongoing improvement and customization.

10. Continuous Learning and Improvement:
- The AI system continuously learns from user interactions and feedback to improve its recipe modification recommendations over time. By analyzing user preferences, dietary trends, and ingredient availability, the system adapts its algorithms to provide more accurate and relevant recommendations for each user.

In summary, AI-driven recipe modification for health or taste preferences involves analyzing existing recipes, incorporating user input, and using machine learning algorithms to generate personalized recommendations for modifying the recipe. By offering tailored adjustments based on user preferences and dietary goals, these systems help users create healthier, tastier meals that align with their individual needs and preferences.

REAL-TIME COOKING GUIDANCE

Real-time cooking guidance and tutorials leverage technology to provide users with step-by-step assistance and instructions during the cooking process. These systems offer interactive support, culinary tips, and demonstrations to help users navigate recipes and cooking techniques more effectively. Here's how real-time cooking guidance and tutorials work:

1. Interactive Recipe Display:
   - Users access recipes through a digital platform, such as a mobile app, smart kitchen device, or website. The recipe is displayed in an interactive format, allowing users to follow along step-by-step as they cook.

2. Video Tutorials:
   - Many real-time cooking guidance systems include video tutorials that demonstrate cooking techniques and procedures. These tutorials provide visual guidance and instruction, making it easier for users to understand each step of the recipe.

3. Voice Guidance:
   - Some systems offer voice-guided instructions that provide real-time feedback and encouragement as users progress through the recipe. Voice guidance can be especially helpful for hands-on cooking tasks that require users to focus on the food rather than a screen.

4. Ingredient Substitution Suggestions:
   - Real-time cooking guidance systems may offer suggestions

for ingredient substitutions based on user preferences, dietary restrictions, or ingredient availability. This ensures that users can adapt recipes to their individual needs without sacrificing flavor or quality.

5. Cooking Tips and Techniques:

- Throughout the cooking process, users receive tips and techniques to improve their culinary skills and enhance the flavor of the dish. These tips may include suggestions for seasoning, temperature control, knife skills, and plating presentation.

6. Cooking Timers and Reminders:

- Real-time cooking guidance systems include built-in timers and reminders to help users keep track of cooking times and avoid overcooking or undercooking their dishes. Users can set timers for each step of the recipe and receive alerts when it's time to move on to the next step.

7. Ingredient Measurement Conversion:

- For users who prefer to cook using metric or imperial measurements, real-time cooking guidance systems offer built-in measurement conversion tools. Users can easily convert ingredient quantities between different units of measurement to ensure accuracy and consistency in their recipes.

8. Nutritional Information:

- Some systems provide nutritional information for each recipe, including calorie counts, macronutrient breakdowns, and allergen information. This helps users make informed choices about their meals and ensure that they align with their dietary goals and preferences.

9. User Feedback and Ratings:

- Users have the opportunity to provide feedback and ratings on recipes they've tried, helping others make informed decisions about which recipes to try. This user-generated content creates a community-driven platform where users can share their cooking experiences and tips with others.

10. Personalized Recommendations:

- Real-time cooking guidance systems offer personalized recipe recommendations based on user preferences, dietary restrictions, and cooking skill level. Users can discover new recipes tailored to their tastes and interests, expanding their culinary repertoire and experimenting with new flavors and cuisines.

In summary, real-time cooking guidance and tutorials provide users with interactive support and instruction as they cook, offering step-by-step guidance, video tutorials, voice guidance, ingredient substitution suggestions, cooking tips, timers, nutritional information, user feedback, and personalized recommendations. By leveraging technology to enhance the cooking experience, these systems empower users to explore new recipes, improve their culinary skills, and enjoy delicious homemade meals with confidence and ease.

ADAPTIVE COOKING TIMERS AND TEMPERATURE CONTROL

Adaptive cooking timers and temperature control systems utilize technology to optimize cooking processes by adjusting cooking times and temperatures based on real-time conditions and user preferences. Here's how these systems work:

1. Sensor Integration:
   - Adaptive cooking systems are equipped with sensors that monitor various parameters such as temperature, humidity, food doneness, and internal food temperatures. These sensors provide real-time data on the cooking environment and the status of the food being cooked.

2. Real-time Monitoring:
   - The sensors continuously monitor the cooking process, providing real-time feedback on the temperature and doneness of the food. This allows the system to make adjustments as needed to ensure that the food is cooked to perfection.

3. Machine Learning Algorithms:
   - Adaptive cooking systems use machine learning algorithms to analyze the sensor data and make predictions about the cooking process. These algorithms learn from past cooking

experiences and user preferences to optimize cooking times and temperatures for different types of food.

4. Adaptive Cooking Timers:

- The system adjusts cooking timers dynamically based on the progress of the cooking process and the desired level of doneness. For example, if the food is cooking faster than expected, the timer may be shortened to prevent overcooking.

5. Temperature Control:

- Adaptive cooking systems control cooking temperatures to ensure that food is cooked evenly and to the desired level of doneness. The system may adjust temperatures in real-time based on factors such as the thickness of the food, the type of cooking method used, and the desired outcome.

6. Customizable Settings:

- Users can customize settings such as cooking preferences, desired doneness levels, and cooking methods to tailor the cooking process to their individual preferences. This allows users to achieve consistent results with their favorite recipes.

7. Alerts and Notifications:

- The system provides alerts and notifications to keep users informed about the progress of the cooking process. Users receive notifications when it's time to check on the food, flip or stir ingredients, or adjust cooking settings.

8. Integration with Smart Devices:

- Adaptive cooking systems may integrate with smart devices such as smartphones, tablets, or smart speakers to provide remote control and monitoring capabilities. Users can monitor the cooking process and make adjustments from anywhere with an internet connection.

9. Recipe Recommendations:

- Some adaptive cooking systems offer recipe recommendations based on user preferences and available ingredients. Users can choose from a selection of curated recipes, and the system will automatically adjust cooking times and temperatures to ensure optimal results.

10. Continuous Learning and Improvement:

- Adaptive cooking systems continuously learn from user feedback and cooking experiences to improve their performance over time. As users interact with the system and provide feedback on the results, the system adjusts its algorithms to better meet their needs and preferences.

In summary, adaptive cooking timers and temperature control systems leverage technology to optimize the cooking process, providing real-time monitoring, dynamic adjustments, customizable settings, alerts and notifications, integration with smart devices, recipe recommendations, and continuous learning and improvement. By adapting to real-time conditions and user preferences, these systems help users achieve consistent, delicious results with their cooking endeavors.

PERSONALIZED NUTRITION RECOMMENDATIONS

Personalized nutrition recommendations leverage technology to provide tailored dietary advice and guidance based on individual health goals, preferences, and dietary requirements. Here's how personalized nutrition recommendations work:

1. User Input:
   - Users provide input regarding their health goals, dietary preferences, lifestyle factors, medical history, and any specific dietary restrictions or requirements they may have.

2. Health Assessment:
   - The system conducts a comprehensive health assessment based on the user's input, analyzing factors such as age, gender, weight, height, activity level, and nutritional needs.

3. Dietary Analysis:
   - Using machine learning algorithms, the system analyzes the user's dietary habits, nutrient intake, and eating patterns to identify areas for improvement and potential nutritional deficiencies.

4. Nutritional Requirements:
   - Based on the user's health assessment and dietary analysis, the system determines their specific nutritional requirements, including recommended daily intake of macronutrients (such

as protein, carbohydrates, and fats), micronutrients (such as vitamins and minerals), and other essential nutrients.

5. Personalized Recommendations:

-   The system generates personalized nutrition recommendations tailored to the user's individual needs and preferences. This may include suggestions for meal planning, portion control, food choices, and dietary modifications to help users achieve their health goals.

6. Recipe Suggestions:

- Personalized nutrition recommendations may include recipe suggestions that align with the user's dietary preferences and nutritional requirements. These recipes are tailored to provide balanced meals that meet the user's specific health goals and taste preferences.

7. Meal Planning:

- The system assists users in creating personalized meal plans that incorporate recommended recipes and food choices. Users can customize their meal plans based on their schedule, budget, and culinary preferences.

8. Nutritional Tracking:

-   Personalized nutrition recommendations systems may include tools for tracking food intake, calorie consumption, and nutrient intake. Users can log their meals and snacks, monitor their nutritional intake in real-time, and receive feedback on their dietary choices.

9. Integration with Wearable Devices:

- Some personalized nutrition recommendation systems integrate with wearable devices such as fitness trackers or smartwatches to track physical activity levels, sleep patterns, and other health metrics. This data is used to further personalize nutrition recommendations and optimize overall health and wellness.

10. Continuous Monitoring and Adjustment:

-   The system continuously monitors the user's progress towards their health goals and adjusts nutrition recommendations accordingly. Users receive regular updates and feedback to help them stay on track and make informed choices about their diet and lifestyle.

In summary, personalized nutrition recommendations leverage technology to provide tailored dietary advice and guidance based on individual health goals, preferences, and dietary requirements. By analyzing user input, conducting health assessments, and generating personalized recommendations, these systems empower users to make informed choices about their diet and nutrition, leading to improved health and wellness outcomes.

TAILORED COOKING EXPERIENCES

Tailored cooking experiences based on user habits and feedback involve leveraging technology to personalize the cooking process according to individual preferences, habits, and feedback. Here's how it works:

1. User Profile Creation:
   - Users create profiles where they input their culinary preferences, dietary restrictions, cooking skill level, favorite ingredients, and any other relevant information.

2. Habit Tracking:
   - The system tracks user habits such as frequently cooked dishes, preferred cooking techniques, preferred meal times, and ingredient usage patterns. This data is used to personalize the cooking experience.

3. Recipe Recommendations:
   - Based on user profiles and habit tracking data, the system recommends recipes that align with the user's preferences and cooking habits. These recommendations may include variations of favorite dishes, new recipes to try, or seasonal recipes featuring preferred ingredients.

4. Customizable Recipes:
   - Users have the option to customize recipes according to their preferences and dietary restrictions. This may include adjusting serving sizes, substituting ingredients, or modifying cooking techniques to suit individual tastes and requirements.

5. Adaptive Cooking Instructions:

- The system provides adaptive cooking instructions that adjust based on user feedback and cooking habits. For example, if a user prefers their steak medium-rare, the system will automatically adjust cooking times and temperatures accordingly.

6. Interactive Cooking Assistance:

- Users receive real-time assistance and guidance throughout the cooking process. This may include step-by-step instructions, video tutorials, cooking tips, and ingredient substitution suggestions to help users achieve the desired results.

7. Feedback Collection:

- After preparing a meal, users provide feedback on the recipe, including taste, texture, difficulty level, and overall satisfaction. This feedback is used to refine future recipe recommendations and improve the cooking experience.

8. Smart Kitchen Appliance Integration:

- The system integrates with smart kitchen appliances to streamline the cooking process. Users can control appliances such as ovens, stoves, and sous vide machines directly from the cooking platform, ensuring precise cooking results.

9. Meal Planning and Grocery List Generation:

- The system assists users in meal planning by suggesting recipes for upcoming meals based on their preferences and habits. It also generates grocery lists based on selected recipes, ensuring users have all the necessary ingredients on hand.

10. Continuous Learning and Improvement:

- The system continuously learns from user interactions, feedback, and cooking experiences to improve its recommendations and personalization over time. This ensures that the cooking experience becomes more tailored and enjoyable for users with each use.

In summary, tailored cooking experiences based on user habits and feedback leverage technology to personalize the cooking process, from recipe recommendations to adaptive cooking instructions and interactive assistance. By incorporating user preferences, habits, and feedback, these systems create a more customized and enjoyable cooking experience for users, helping them achieve delicious results with confidence and ease.

INTEROPERABILITY WITH OTHER SMART HOME DEVICES

Integration with the smart home ecosystem involves ensuring interoperability between kitchen devices and other smart home devices to create a seamless and interconnected experience. Here's how integration with other smart home devices works:

1. Communication Protocols:
   - Smart kitchen devices utilize communication protocols such as Wi-Fi, Bluetooth, Zigbee, or Z-Wave to connect with other smart home devices. These protocols enable seamless communication and data exchange between devices.

2. Centralized Control Hub:
   - Many smart home ecosystems include a centralized control hub or platform that serves as a hub for managing all connected devices. This hub allows users to control and monitor their smart kitchen devices alongside other smart home devices from a single interface.

3. Voice Assistants Integration:
   - Smart kitchen devices integrate with popular voice assistants like Amazon Alexa, Google Assistant, or Apple Siri, allowing users to control them using voice commands. Users can ask the voice assistant to preheat the oven, adjust the stove temperature, or start a coffee maker without needing to manually operate the devices.

4. Cross-Device Automation:

- Integration with other smart home devices enables cross-device automation and coordination. For example, users can create automation routines that trigger specific actions based on predefined conditions or events. This could include turning on kitchen lights when the oven is in use or adjusting the thermostat when the kitchen temperature rises.

5. Energy Management:

- Smart home ecosystems often include energy management features that help users optimize energy usage and reduce utility bills. Integration with smart kitchen devices allows users to monitor energy consumption, schedule appliance usage during off-peak hours, and receive insights on energy-efficient cooking practices.

6. Security and Monitoring:

- Integration with smart home security systems allows users to monitor their kitchen remotely and receive alerts in case of any security breaches or safety concerns. This could include detecting smoke or carbon monoxide alarms, monitoring for leaks or floods, or checking the status of kitchen appliances when away from home.

7. Scene Control:

- Users can create customized scenes or presets that trigger a series of actions across multiple smart home devices with a single command. For example, a "cooking" scene could dim the lights, turn on the range hood, and play background music to create the perfect ambiance for cooking.

8. Data Sharing and Insights:

- Integration with other smart home devices allows for data sharing and insights that help users make informed decisions about their kitchen activities. For example, data from smart kitchen devices could be used to track cooking habits, monitor food inventory, or analyze energy usage patterns.

9. Mobile App Integration:

- Smart kitchen devices often come with companion mobile apps that allow users to control and monitor their devices remotely. Integration with other smart home devices may extend the functionality of these apps, providing users with a unified interface for managing all connected devices.

10. Expandability and Compatibility:

- Smart home ecosystems are designed to be expandable and compatible with a wide range of devices from different manufacturers. This ensures that users can easily add new devices to their smart home setup and enjoy seamless interoperability between all connected devices.

In summary, integration with the smart home ecosystem enables interoperability between kitchen devices and other smart home devices, allowing users to control and monitor their kitchen appliances alongside other connected devices from a centralized interface. By leveraging communication protocols, voice assistants, automation features, energy management tools, security systems, and data sharing capabilities, integration with the smart home ecosystem enhances the functionality and convenience of smart kitchen devices, creating a more efficient and interconnected home environment.

COHESIVE SMART HOME ECOSYSTEM

Creating a cohesive smart home ecosystem centered around the kitchen involves integrating various smart devices and technologies to streamline kitchen tasks, enhance convenience, and improve overall functionality. Here's how to achieve this:

1. Smart Kitchen Appliances:
   - Start by integrating smart kitchen appliances such as refrigerators, ovens, stoves, dishwashers, and coffee makers. These appliances should be equipped with Wi-Fi connectivity and compatible with your smart home ecosystem.

2. Voice Assistants Integration:
   - Integrate voice assistants like Amazon Alexa, Google Assistant, or Apple Siri into your smart home ecosystem. Voice assistants allow for hands-free control of kitchen devices, recipe recommendations, and other tasks.

3. Smart Lighting:
   - Install smart lighting systems in your kitchen that can be controlled remotely or automated based on time of day or activity. Adjusting lighting can enhance ambiance, improve visibility, and create a more comfortable cooking environment.

4. Smart Thermostat:
   - Incorporate a smart thermostat into your kitchen to control heating and cooling systems. This allows for energy-efficient temperature management and ensures comfort while cooking and dining.

5. Smart Sensors:

- Deploy smart sensors in the kitchen to monitor environmental factors such as temperature, humidity, and air quality. These sensors can provide valuable insights and automate tasks like ventilation or adjusting appliance settings.

6. Smart Security Cameras:

- Install smart security cameras in the kitchen area to monitor activity, detect intruders, or check on cooking progress remotely. Integrating cameras with your smart home ecosystem enhances kitchen security and provides peace of mind.

7. Smart Displays or Tablets:

- Place smart displays or tablets in the kitchen for quick access to recipes, cooking tutorials, and smart home controls. These devices can also display calendar events, weather updates, and reminders.

8. Meal Planning and Grocery Management:

- Use meal planning and grocery management apps that integrate with your smart home ecosystem. Plan meals, create shopping lists, and receive recipe suggestions based on ingredients you have on hand or dietary preferences.

9. Smart Kitchen Gadgets:

- Consider adding smart kitchen gadgets such as scales, thermometers, or timers that can connect to your smart home ecosystem. These gadgets provide accurate measurements, monitor cooking progress, and enhance cooking precision.

10. Automation and Scenes:

- Set up automation routines and scenes to streamline kitchen tasks and create personalized experiences. For example, you could create a "morning routine" scene that starts the coffee maker, adjusts the thermostat, and turns on the kitchen lights when you wake up.

11. Data Integration and Insights:

- Integrate data from your smart kitchen devices into a centralized dashboard or app that provides insights and analytics. Monitor energy usage, track cooking habits, and receive recommendations for optimizing kitchen efficiency.

12. Expandability and Compatibility:

- Ensure that your smart home ecosystem is expandable and compatible with a wide range of devices and platforms. This allows you to add new devices and functionalities as needed, ensuring flexibility and scalability over time.

By integrating these components into a cohesive smart home ecosystem centered around the kitchen, you can create a more efficient, convenient, and enjoyable cooking and dining experience. Whether you're preparing meals, entertaining guests, or simply relaxing with family, a well-designed smart kitchen ecosystem enhances every aspect of the culinary journey.

PRIVACY CONCERNS

Privacy concerns with AI-powered kitchen devices arise from the collection, storage, and use of personal data generated by these devices. Here are some of the key challenges and ethical considerations:

1. Data Collection and Storage:
   - AI-powered kitchen devices collect a vast amount of data, including user interactions, cooking habits, dietary preferences, and even audio or video recordings. Storing this data raises concerns about unauthorized access, data breaches, and misuse of personal information.

2. Surveillance and Monitoring:
   - Smart kitchen devices with audio or video capabilities may inadvertently invade users' privacy by monitoring activities in the kitchen without their consent. Users may feel uncomfortable with the idea of being under constant surveillance, especially in private spaces like their homes.

3. Data Security and Protection:
   - Ensuring the security and protection of personal data is paramount to addressing privacy concerns. AI-powered kitchen devices must implement robust security measures, such as encryption, authentication, and access controls, to safeguard sensitive information from unauthorized access or hacking attempts.

4. Consent and Transparency:
   - Users should be fully informed about the data collection practices of AI-powered kitchen devices and have the

opportunity to provide explicit consent before their data is collected or used. Transparency about how data is collected, stored, and shared is essential for building trust with users.

5. Data Ownership and Control:

- Users should retain ownership and control over their personal data collected by AI-powered kitchen devices. They should have the ability to access, modify, or delete their data as desired, and have clear mechanisms for exercising their data rights.

6. Third-party Sharing and Integration:

- AI-powered kitchen devices may share data with third-party services, such as recipe apps, grocery delivery services, or advertising networks, for various purposes. Users should be aware of these data-sharing practices and have the option to opt out if they choose.

7. Bias and Discrimination:

- AI algorithms used in kitchen devices may inadvertently perpetuate biases or discrimination, particularly in areas such as recipe recommendations or nutritional advice. Developers must carefully design and test algorithms to mitigate bias and ensure fair and equitable outcomes for all users.

8. Children's Privacy:

- Special considerations should be given to children's privacy when designing AI-powered kitchen devices, as children may interact with these devices unsupervised. Developers should comply with regulations such as the Children's Online Privacy Protection Act (COPPA) and implement additional safeguards to protect children's privacy rights.

9. Ethical Use of Data:

- Companies that develop AI-powered kitchen devices have a responsibility to use personal data ethically and responsibly. They should prioritize user privacy and data protection, avoid intrusive data collection practices, and use data only for legitimate purposes that benefit users.

10. Regulatory Compliance:

- AI-powered kitchen devices must comply with relevant privacy laws and regulations, such as the General Data Protection Regulation (GDPR) in the European Union or the California Consumer Privacy Act (CCPA) in the United States. Compliance with these regulations helps ensure that user privacy rights are respected and protected.

Addressing privacy concerns with AI-powered kitchen devices requires a comprehensive approach that prioritizes user privacy, transparency, consent, data security, and ethical use of data. By implementing robust privacy measures and respecting user rights, developers can build trust with users and foster a positive relationship between consumers and technology.

POTENTIAL BIASES

Potential biases in AI algorithms related to food and cooking can arise from various sources and may have ethical implications. Here are some challenges and ethical considerations:

1. Cultural Bias in Recipe Recommendations:
   - AI algorithms that recommend recipes may exhibit cultural bias, favoring certain cuisines or ingredients over others. This bias can reflect the cultural background of the developers or the training data used to train the algorithm, potentially marginalizing or excluding cuisines from underrepresented cultures.

2. Nutritional Bias in Dietary Recommendations:
   - AI algorithms that provide dietary recommendations may exhibit bias towards certain nutritional guidelines or dietary trends, potentially promoting diets that are not suitable for all individuals. For example, algorithms biased towards low-carb diets may not adequately consider the nutritional needs of individuals with specific health conditions or cultural dietary preferences.

3. Ingredient Bias in Recipe Generation:
   - AI algorithms that generate recipes may exhibit bias towards common or popular ingredients, overlooking lesser-known or culturally-specific ingredients. This bias can limit the diversity of recipes generated by the algorithm and perpetuate food trends at the expense of culinary diversity.

4. Gender Bias in Cooking Assistance:

- AI-powered cooking assistants may exhibit gender bias in their interactions with users, such as using gendered language or stereotypes when providing cooking tips or instructions. This bias can reinforce traditional gender roles and expectations, potentially alienating users who do not conform to these norms.

5. Socioeconomic Bias in Ingredient Recommendations:

- AI algorithms that recommend ingredients for recipes may exhibit bias towards expensive or exotic ingredients, assuming that users have the means to afford them. This bias can overlook the economic constraints faced by users with limited financial resources, potentially excluding them from accessing certain recipes or ingredients.

6. Accessibility Bias in Cooking Instructions:

- AI-powered cooking assistants may exhibit bias in their instructions, assuming a certain level of culinary skill or access to specialized equipment. This bias can disadvantage users with disabilities or limited cooking experience, making it difficult for them to follow the instructions effectively.

7. Environmental Bias in Food Choices:

- AI algorithms that recommend food choices may exhibit bias towards environmentally unsustainable or ethically questionable ingredients, such as those associated with deforestation, habitat destruction, or animal cruelty. This bias can perpetuate harmful practices in the food industry and undermine efforts towards sustainability and ethical consumption.

8. Health Bias in Recipe Modification:

- AI algorithms that modify recipes for health purposes may exhibit bias towards certain dietary guidelines or nutritional theories, potentially overlooking individual health needs or preferences. This bias can lead to recommendations that are not aligned with the user's health goals or may even be harmful to their well-being.

9. Representation Bias in Culinary Content:
   - AI algorithms that curate culinary content, such as recipe websites or cooking videos, may exhibit bias towards content created by individuals or organizations with greater visibility or influence. This bias can marginalize lesser-known creators or communities, limiting their representation in the culinary space.

10. Mitigating Bias and Ensuring Ethical AI:
   - Developers and researchers must actively work to identify and mitigate biases in AI algorithms related to food and cooking. This includes diversifying training data, incorporating diverse perspectives in algorithm development, conducting bias assessments, and implementing fairness-aware AI techniques to ensure equitable outcomes for all users.

Addressing potential biases in AI algorithms related to food and cooking requires a concerted effort to promote diversity, inclusion, and fairness in algorithm development and deployment. By recognizing and addressing biases, developers can build AI systems that provide more equitable, culturally sensitive, and inclusive experiences for users in the culinary domain.

ENVIRONMENTAL IMPACT AND SUSTAINABILITY CONSIDERATIONS

Environmental impact and sustainability considerations are crucial when developing and using AI-powered kitchen devices. Here are some challenges and ethical considerations related to this:

1. Energy Consumption:
   - AI-powered kitchen devices can consume significant amounts of energy, especially if they are constantly connected to the internet or utilize complex algorithms. Minimizing energy consumption through efficient design and optimization is essential to reduce the environmental footprint of these devices.

2. Electronic Waste:
   - The rapid turnover of technology and the proliferation of smart kitchen devices contribute to electronic waste accumulation. Manufacturers should prioritize durability, repairability, and recyclability in device design to minimize the environmental impact of disposal.

3. Sustainable Sourcing of Materials:
   - The materials used in the manufacturing of AI-

powered kitchen devices should be sourced responsibly, prioritizing renewable resources, recycled materials, and non-toxic components. Sustainable sourcing practices help reduce environmental degradation and support ethical supply chains.

4. Lifecycle Assessment:

- Conducting a lifecycle assessment of AI-powered kitchen devices helps evaluate their environmental impact from production to disposal. This assessment considers factors such as raw material extraction, manufacturing processes, transportation, usage phase, and end-of-life disposal, guiding efforts to minimize environmental harm at each stage.

5. Carbon Footprint Reduction:

- Implementing measures to reduce the carbon footprint of AI-powered kitchen devices is essential for mitigating climate change. This includes optimizing energy efficiency, promoting renewable energy use, and offsetting emissions through carbon-neutral initiatives.

6. Food Waste Reduction:

- AI-powered kitchen devices can play a role in reducing food waste by optimizing meal planning, ingredient management, and cooking efficiency. By minimizing food waste, these devices help conserve natural resources, reduce greenhouse gas emissions, and alleviate pressure on landfills.

7. Sustainable Food Choices:

- AI algorithms that recommend recipes or meal plans should prioritize sustainable and environmentally friendly food choices. This includes promoting plant-based diets, sourcing local and seasonal ingredients, and reducing the consumption of resource-intensive foods such as meat and dairy products.

8. Environmental Education and Awareness:

- Educating users about the environmental impact of their food choices and kitchen practices helps foster awareness and encourage sustainable behaviors. AI-powered kitchen devices can provide insights, tips, and recommendations for environmentally conscious cooking and consumption.

9. Ethical Sourcing and Fair Trade Practices:

- AI-powered kitchen devices should support ethical sourcing and fair trade practices by promoting transparency in the supply chain and ensuring that ingredients are sourced from producers who adhere to sustainable and ethical standards. This includes avoiding ingredients associated with deforestation, habitat destruction, or labor exploitation.

10. Collaboration and Partnerships:

- Collaboration between technology companies, environmental organizations, and policymakers is essential for addressing sustainability challenges in the development and deployment of AI-powered kitchen devices. By working together, stakeholders can develop innovative solutions, advocate for policy changes, and promote sustainable practices across the industry.

In summary, addressing environmental impact and sustainability considerations in the development and use of AI-powered kitchen devices requires a holistic approach that considers energy efficiency, material sourcing, lifecycle assessment, carbon footprint reduction, food waste reduction, sustainable food choices, environmental education, ethical sourcing, and collaboration among stakeholders. By prioritizing sustainability principles in device design, operation, and user engagement, AI-powered kitchen devices can contribute to a more environmentally friendly and sustainable future.

PREDICTING THE FUTURE OF AI IN THE KITCHEN

Predicting the future of AI in the kitchen involves envisioning how technological advancements and societal trends will shape the way we cook, eat, and interact with our kitchen spaces. Here are some predictions for future trends and possibilities:

1. Personalized Culinary Experiences:
   - AI algorithms will become increasingly adept at understanding individual preferences, dietary restrictions, and culinary skills, allowing for highly personalized cooking experiences. Smart kitchen devices will offer tailored recipe recommendations, adaptive cooking instructions, and customized meal plans based on user profiles and feedback.

2. Seamless Integration with Smart Home Ecosystems:
   - AI-powered kitchen devices will seamlessly integrate with other smart home devices and platforms, creating a cohesive and interconnected home environment. Users will be able to control kitchen appliances, access recipes, and manage meal planning through voice commands, mobile apps, or centralized smart home hubs.

3. Enhanced Automation and Efficiency:
   - Automation technologies such as robotic chefs, automated cooking appliances, and smart kitchen assistants will

streamline kitchen tasks and enhance cooking efficiency. These technologies will handle repetitive or labor-intensive tasks, freeing up time for users to focus on creativity and culinary experimentation.

4. Sustainable Cooking Practices:

- AI algorithms will promote sustainable cooking practices by recommending environmentally friendly ingredients, reducing food waste, and optimizing energy usage. Smart kitchen devices will provide insights and suggestions for minimizing environmental impact while preparing delicious and nutritious meals.

5. Culinary Education and Skill Development:

- AI-powered kitchen platforms will serve as virtual culinary instructors, offering cooking tutorials, skill-building exercises, and interactive cooking classes. Users will have access to a wealth of educational resources and guidance to enhance their culinary skills and confidence in the kitchen.

6. Hyper-Personalized Nutrition Solutions:

- AI algorithms will deliver hyper-personalized nutrition solutions tailored to individual health goals, dietary preferences, and genetic profiles. Smart kitchen devices will analyze nutritional needs, track dietary intake, and provide real-time feedback and recommendations to optimize health and well-being.

7. Multimodal Cooking Interfaces:

- Future kitchen interfaces will incorporate multimodal interaction methods, combining voice commands, gesture recognition, touchscreens, and augmented reality (AR) interfaces. Users will interact with kitchen devices using natural and intuitive interfaces, enhancing user experience and accessibility.

8. Culinary Creativity and Innovation:

- AI algorithms will inspire culinary creativity and innovation by generating novel recipes, exploring flavor combinations, and experimenting with cultural fusion cuisines. Smart kitchen devices will serve as creative collaborators, sparking inspiration and pushing the boundaries of gastronomic exploration.

9. Culinary Tourism and Global Cuisine Exploration:
  - AI-powered culinary platforms will facilitate virtual culinary experiences, allowing users to explore global cuisines, discover authentic recipes, and connect with chefs and food enthusiasts from around the world. Culinary tourism will transcend geographical boundaries, offering immersive gastronomic experiences from the comfort of home.

10. Ethical and Cultural Considerations:
  - As AI technologies play an increasingly prominent role in the kitchen, ethical and cultural considerations will become paramount. Developers, users, and policymakers will collaborate to ensure that AI-powered kitchen solutions prioritize inclusivity, diversity, sustainability, and ethical practices, reflecting the values and preferences of diverse communities.

In summary, the future of AI in the kitchen holds exciting possibilities for personalized culinary experiences, seamless integration with smart home ecosystems, enhanced automation and efficiency, sustainable cooking practices, culinary education and skill development, hyper-personalized nutrition solutions, multimodal cooking interfaces, culinary creativity and innovation, culinary tourism, and ethical and cultural considerations. By harnessing the power of AI technologies responsibly and ethically, we can create a future where cooking is not only convenient and efficient but also creative, sustainable, and culturally enriching.

EMERGING TECHNOLOGIES AND INNOVATIONS

Emerging technologies and innovations are poised to revolutionize the way we cook, eat, and interact with our kitchen spaces. Here are some future trends and possibilities in the realm of kitchen technology:

1. 3D Food Printing:
   - 3D food printing technology allows for the creation of intricate food designs and customized shapes using edible materials. In the future, 3D food printers may become commonplace in kitchens, enabling personalized food creations, artistic presentations, and novel culinary experiences.

2. Smart Food Packaging:
   - Smart food packaging equipped with sensors and RFID tags will provide real-time information about food freshness, expiration dates, and nutritional content. These packaging solutions will help reduce food waste, ensure food safety, and enhance consumer confidence in the products they purchase.

3. Augmented Reality (AR) Cooking Assistance:
   - AR technologies will provide immersive cooking assistance, overlaying virtual instructions, recipe steps, and cooking tips onto the physical kitchen environment. Users will receive real-time guidance and visual cues as they navigate the cooking process, improving accuracy and efficiency in the kitchen.

4. Internet of Things (IoT) Kitchen Ecosystems:
   - IoT-enabled kitchen ecosystems will connect appliances, devices, and sensors to create smart and interconnected cooking environments. Users will control and monitor their kitchen appliances remotely, automate cooking tasks, and receive personalized recommendations based on their preferences and habits.

5. Biometric Food Analysis:
   - Biometric sensors and spectroscopy techniques will allow for non-invasive analysis of food composition, quality, and safety. Users will be able to assess the nutritional content, freshness, and authenticity of food items using handheld devices or smartphone apps, empowering them to make informed food choices.

6. Molecular Gastronomy Tools:
   - Molecular gastronomy tools and techniques will transition from professional kitchens to home settings, enabling amateur chefs to experiment with avant-garde culinary creations. Tools such as sous vide machines, rotary evaporators, and spherification kits will become more accessible and affordable to consumers.

7. Blockchain Traceability in Food Supply Chains:
   - Blockchain technology will enhance transparency and traceability in food supply chains, allowing consumers to verify the origin, authenticity, and sustainability of food products. Blockchain-based platforms will enable farmers, producers, and retailers to track the journey of food from farm to fork, fostering trust and accountability in the food industry.

8. Plant-Based Alternatives and Cultured Meat:
   - Advances in food science and biotechnology will lead to the development of more realistic plant-based alternatives and cultured meat products. These alternatives will offer environmentally sustainable and ethically sourced protein

options, catering to consumers' growing interest in plant-forward diets and ethical eating.

9. Quantum Computing for Food Optimization:

- Quantum computing technology will revolutionize food optimization and recipe formulation by solving complex optimization problems at unprecedented speeds. Quantum algorithms will enable chefs and food scientists to design novel recipes, optimize ingredient combinations, and explore new culinary frontiers.

10. AI-Powered Flavor Profiling and Generation:

- AI algorithms will analyze flavor profiles, ingredient interactions, and culinary trends to generate novel flavor combinations and recipe recommendations. These algorithms will leverage machine learning techniques to understand user preferences and create personalized culinary experiences tailored to individual tastes.

In summary, emerging technologies and innovations in the kitchen space hold tremendous potential to transform the way we cook, eat, and engage with food. From 3D food printing and smart food packaging to AR cooking assistance and blockchain traceability, these advancements will enhance convenience, creativity, sustainability, and safety in the kitchen, ushering in a new era of culinary exploration and innovation.

OPPORTUNITIES FOR FURTHER RESEARCH AND DEVELOPMENT

Opportunities for further research and development in the field of kitchen technology abound, driven by the increasing integration of AI, IoT, and advanced materials into culinary processes. Here are some key areas where research and development efforts can make a significant impact:

1. AI-Driven Culinary Creativity:
   - Further research into AI-driven culinary creativity can explore how machine learning algorithms can assist chefs and home cooks in developing innovative recipes, flavor combinations, and cooking techniques. This research can encompass natural language processing, deep learning, and generative models to understand and generate novel culinary content.

2. Sustainable Food Systems:
   - Research and development initiatives focused on sustainable food systems can investigate technologies and practices that promote food security, reduce food waste, and minimize environmental impact. This may include advancements in precision agriculture, vertical farming, aquaponics, and regenerative agriculture to produce nutritious food in an environmentally friendly manner.

3. Food Safety and Quality Assurance:

- Advances in food safety and quality assurance research can explore sensor technologies, spectroscopy techniques, and blockchain solutions to ensure the safety, authenticity, and traceability of food products throughout the supply chain. This research can enhance food safety standards, mitigate foodborne illnesses, and improve consumer confidence in the food industry.

4. Personalized Nutrition and Health:
- Research into personalized nutrition and health can leverage AI algorithms, genetic analysis, and biomarker profiling to develop personalized dietary recommendations and interventions tailored to individual health goals, genetic predispositions, and metabolic profiles. This research can optimize nutrition outcomes, prevent chronic diseases, and promote overall well-being.

5. Human-Robot Collaboration in the Kitchen:
- Further exploration of human-robot collaboration in the kitchen can investigate how robotic systems can assist humans in complex cooking tasks, food preparation, and kitchen management. This research can focus on human-robot interaction, task allocation, and collaborative planning to enhance efficiency and creativity in culinary workflows.

6. Multisensory Food Experiences:
- Research into multisensory food experiences can explore how technology can enhance the sensory aspects of food consumption, including taste, aroma, texture, and presentation. This may involve virtual reality (VR) simulations, haptic feedback systems, and aroma delivery devices to create immersive dining experiences that stimulate all the senses.

7. Cultural and Ethical Considerations:
- Research initiatives that consider cultural and ethical dimensions of food technology can investigate how technology can respect and preserve cultural culinary traditions, promote

food sovereignty, and address ethical concerns related to food production and consumption. This research can foster inclusivity, diversity, and sustainability in the culinary domain.

8. Kitchen Ergonomics and Accessibility:

- Further research into kitchen ergonomics and accessibility can explore how kitchen design, layout, and equipment can be optimized to accommodate individuals with disabilities, mobility challenges, or special dietary needs. This research can promote universal design principles, assistive technologies, and inclusive culinary experiences for all users.

9. Data-Driven Culinary Insights:

- Research on data-driven culinary insights can analyze large-scale food data sets, social media trends, and user preferences to uncover insights into culinary preferences, cultural food practices, and emerging food trends. This research can inform recipe development, menu planning, and food marketing strategies in the food industry.

10. Interdisciplinary Collaborations:

- Encouraging interdisciplinary collaborations between culinary experts, food scientists, engineers, designers, and social scientists can foster innovation and creativity in kitchen technology research and development. By bringing together diverse perspectives and expertise, these collaborations can tackle complex challenges and drive meaningful advancements in the field.

In summary, opportunities for further research and development in kitchen technology abound, spanning AI-driven culinary creativity, sustainable food systems, food safety and quality assurance, personalized nutrition and health, human-robot collaboration, multisensory food experiences, cultural and ethical considerations, kitchen ergonomics and accessibility, data-driven culinary insights, and interdisciplinary collaborations. By prioritizing these areas of research, the culinary technology community can contribute to the advancement of innovative, sustainable, and inclusive solutions that enhance the way we cook, eat, and engage with food in the future.

SUCCESS STORIES

Success stories in the realm of kitchen technology highlight the transformative impact of innovation and technological advancements on culinary experiences. Here are a few notable success stories:

1. June Oven:

- June, a smart countertop oven, utilizes AI and computer vision technology to automatically recognize and cook food items to perfection. With features such as food recognition, temperature monitoring, and recipe suggestions, June Oven has garnered acclaim for its ability to simplify cooking tasks and produce restaurant-quality results at home.

2. Drop Kitchen Scale:

- Drop is a smart kitchen scale that pairs with a mobile app to guide users through step-by-step cooking instructions and recipe adjustments. By precisely measuring ingredients and providing real-time feedback, Drop helps users achieve consistent and delicious results, making cooking more accessible and enjoyable for home cooks of all skill levels.

3. Nomiku Sous Vide Immersion Circulator:

- Nomiku revolutionized home cooking with its sous vide immersion circulator, which allows users to cook restaurant-quality meals with precision and ease. By circulating water at a precise temperature, Nomiku ensures even cooking and optimal flavor retention, resulting in tender, flavorful dishes that rival those of professional chefs.

4. Anova Precision Cooker:

- Anova's precision cooker is another popular sous vide device that has gained widespread acclaim for its simplicity and reliability. With features such as Wi-Fi connectivity, temperature control, and recipe customization, Anova empowers home cooks to experiment with sous vide cooking techniques and achieve restaurant-quality results from the comfort of their kitchens.

5. Whirlpool Smart Kitchen Appliances:
- Whirlpool has introduced a range of smart kitchen appliances equipped with advanced features such as voice control, remote monitoring, and adaptive cooking algorithms. With innovations such as smart refrigerators, ovens, and dishwashers, Whirlpool is redefining the kitchen experience, offering convenience, efficiency, and connectivity to modern households.

6. Innit Platform:
- Innit is a comprehensive culinary platform that integrates recipe discovery, meal planning, grocery shopping, and cooking guidance into a seamless digital experience. By leveraging AI and machine learning, Innit provides personalized recommendations, adaptive cooking instructions, and nutritional insights, empowering users to make informed food choices and enjoy delicious meals at home.

7. Hestan Cue Smart Cooking System:
- Hestan Cue combines smart cookware, induction cooktop, and mobile app to offer a guided cooking experience that helps users master a wide range of recipes and cooking techniques. With features such as temperature control, recipe synchronization, and step-by-step video guidance, Hestan Cue simplifies the cooking process and enables users to create restaurant-quality dishes with confidence.

8. Samsung Family Hub Refrigerator:
- Samsung's Family Hub refrigerator is equipped with a range

of smart features, including a built-in touchscreen display, voice control, and internet connectivity. With features such as recipe suggestions, meal planning, and grocery management, Family Hub transforms the refrigerator into a central hub for kitchen organization, communication, and entertainment.

9. Perfect Company's Perfect Blend Smart Scale:
   - Perfect Blend is a smart scale designed for precision blending and recipe customization. By pairing with a mobile app, Perfect Blend guides users through recipe creation, ingredient measurement, and nutritional analysis, ensuring accurate and delicious smoothies, soups, and sauces every time.

10. Brava Smart Oven:
   - Brava is a countertop smart oven that uses light technology to cook food quickly and efficiently. With features such as precision cooking zones, recipe pre-programming, and remote monitoring, Brava offers a versatile and convenient cooking solution for busy households, enabling users to prepare a wide range of dishes with ease.

Sure, here are a few more success stories in the realm of kitchen technology:

11. Instant Pot:
   - Instant Pot has become a household name with its multi-functional electric pressure cookers that offer a variety of cooking methods in one appliance. With features such as pressure cooking, slow cooking, sautéing, and steaming, Instant Pot has revolutionized meal preparation, making it faster, easier, and more convenient for home cooks.

12. Meater:
   - Meater is a wireless smart meat thermometer that allows users to monitor the internal temperature of meat remotely using a smartphone app. With features such as temperature alerts, cooking notifications, and recipe recommendations, Meater ensures perfectly cooked meat every time, eliminating

the guesswork and ensuring consistent results.

13. Bartesian Cocktail Machine:
   - Bartesian is a cocktail machine that offers a convenient way to enjoy expertly crafted cocktails at home. By using pre-mixed cocktail capsules and customizable strength settings, Bartesian delivers bar-quality cocktails with the push of a button, allowing users to entertain guests or unwind after a long day with their favorite drinks.

14. Tovala Smart Oven:
   - Tovala is a smart oven that combines steam cooking technology with a meal delivery service to offer convenient and healthy meals at home. With features such as barcode scanning, meal customization, and remote control, Tovala simplifies meal preparation and provides users with delicious, chef-crafted meals with minimal effort.

15. Amazon Dash Wand:
   - Amazon Dash Wand is a handheld device equipped with voice recognition and barcode scanning capabilities that allows users to quickly add items to their shopping cart or create grocery lists. With features such as voice ordering, recipe recommendations, and delivery integration, Dash Wand streamlines the shopping experience and makes it easier for users to stock their kitchens with essentials.

16. PerfectBake Smart Scale:
   - PerfectBake is a smart scale designed specifically for baking enthusiasts, offering precise measurement and recipe guidance for a variety of baked goods. With features such as ingredient scaling, step-by-step instructions, and automatic conversion, PerfectBake helps users achieve consistent and delicious results in their baking endeavors.

17. ChefSteps Joule Sous Vide:
   - ChefSteps Joule is a compact and powerful sous vide immersion circulator that offers precise temperature control

and intuitive operation. With features such as smartphone connectivity, recipe sharing, and visual doneness indicators, Joule simplifies sous vide cooking and empowers users to create restaurant-quality meals at home.

18. Mellow Smart Sous Vide:

- Mellow is a smart sous vide machine that combines precise temperature control with refrigeration to ensure food is cooked to perfection and kept fresh until ready to eat. With features such as meal planning, scheduling, and remote control, Mellow offers a convenient and customizable cooking experience for busy individuals and families.

19. Traeger Smart Grills:

- Traeger's line of smart grills offers wood-fired flavor with the convenience of modern technology. With features such as Wi-Fi connectivity, temperature monitoring, and recipe integration, Traeger smart grills make it easy to achieve delicious barbecue results every time, whether grilling, smoking, or baking.

20. Brava Chef Oven:

- Brava Chef Oven is a countertop smart oven that uses light technology to cook food quickly and efficiently. With features such as precision cooking zones, recipe pre-programming, and remote monitoring, Brava Chef Oven offers a versatile and convenient cooking solution for busy households, enabling users to prepare a wide range of dishes with ease.

These success stories demonstrate the transformative potential of kitchen technology in enhancing culinary experiences, simplifying cooking tasks, and empowering users to explore new flavors and techniques in the kitchen. By leveraging innovations in AI, IoT, and smart appliances, these companies have reimagined the kitchen as a hub of creativity, convenience, and connection, inspiring home cooks around the world to discover the joy of cooking.

LESSONS LEARNT

From the success stories and advancements in kitchen technology, several valuable lessons can be learned:

1. User-Centric Design:
   - Successful kitchen technologies prioritize user experience, offering intuitive interfaces, convenient features, and seamless integration into users' lifestyles. User-centric design ensures that technology enhances, rather than complicates, the cooking experience.

2. Innovation Through Integration:
   - Integrating multiple technologies, such as AI, IoT, and smart appliances, allows for comprehensive solutions that address various aspects of cooking, from recipe planning to ingredient sourcing. Combining technologies leads to more robust and versatile kitchen solutions.

3. Simplification of Complex Processes:
   - Technologies that simplify complex cooking tasks, such as precise temperature control in sous vide cooking or automated recipe adjustments based on ingredient measurements, make cooking more accessible and enjoyable for users of all skill levels.

4. Focus on Convenience and Efficiency:
   - Kitchen technologies that prioritize convenience, such as remote monitoring, pre-programmed recipes, and automated cooking processes, resonate with busy consumers seeking efficient solutions that fit into their hectic lifestyles.

5. Empowerment Through Education:

- Technologies that offer educational resources, such as cooking tutorials, recipe recommendations, and nutritional insights, empower users to expand their culinary skills, experiment with new flavors, and make informed food choices.

6. Sustainability and Environmental Responsibility:
- Technologies that promote sustainability, such as reducing food waste, optimizing energy usage, and supporting ethical sourcing practices, align with consumers' growing concern for environmental impact and ethical food production.

7. Flexibility and Adaptability:
- Flexible technologies that accommodate diverse cooking styles, dietary preferences, and cultural cuisines appeal to a wide range of users, allowing for personalized culinary experiences tailored to individual tastes and preferences.

8. Collaboration and Interdisciplinary Innovation:
- Collaboration between culinary experts, technologists, designers, and researchers drives innovation and fosters the development of holistic solutions that address the multifaceted challenges of modern cooking.

9. Continuous Improvement and Iteration:
- Successful kitchen technologies undergo continuous improvement and iteration based on user feedback, technological advancements, and changing consumer preferences. Iterative development ensures that technology remains relevant, reliable, and responsive to users' needs.

10. Ethical Considerations and Social Impact:
- Technologies that consider ethical considerations, such as cultural sensitivity, privacy protection, and inclusivity, build trust with users and contribute to positive social impact by promoting diversity, equity, and accessibility in the culinary domain.

Overall, the lessons learned from success stories in kitchen technology underscore the importance of designing technology that enhances the cooking experience, empowers users, promotes sustainability, fosters collaboration, and prioritizes ethical considerations. By applying these lessons, developers and innovators can create kitchen technologies that inspire creativity, simplify cooking tasks, and enrich the culinary journey for users around the world.

CASE STUDY: PERFECTBAKE SMART SCALE - REVOLUTIONIZING BAKING EXPERIENCES

Background:
PerfectBake is a leading manufacturer of smart kitchen appliances, dedicated to enhancing the cooking experience through innovative technology. In response to the growing demand for precision baking tools, PerfectBake developed the PerfectBake Smart Scale, a revolutionary kitchen device designed to empower home bakers with precise measurement and recipe guidance.

Challenge:
Baking is a precise art that requires accurate measurement of ingredients to achieve consistent and delicious results. However, many home bakers struggle with imprecise measuring tools and lack of recipe guidance, leading to inconsistent outcomes and frustration in the kitchen. PerfectBake identified an opportunity to address these challenges by developing a smart scale that combines precision measurement with intelligent recipe assistance to streamline the baking process and inspire confidence in home bakers.

Solution:

The PerfectBake Smart Scale is a compact and versatile kitchen device equipped with advanced features to simplify the baking experience. Key features of the PerfectBake Smart Scale include:

1. Precision Measurement: The smart scale offers precise measurement of ingredients in grams, ounces, pounds, and milliliters, ensuring accuracy and consistency in baking recipes.

2. Intelligent Recipe Guidance: Paired with a mobile app, the smart scale provides step-by-step recipe guidance, including ingredient scaling, mixing instructions, and baking times. The app offers a wide range of recipes curated by professional bakers and allows users to customize recipes based on dietary preferences and ingredient availability.

3. Ingredient Substitution: The app includes a database of ingredient substitutions, allowing users to easily replace ingredients based on dietary restrictions or pantry availability without compromising the integrity of the recipe.

4. Nutritional Analysis: The smart scale provides nutritional analysis of recipes, including calorie count, macronutrient breakdown, and allergen information, empowering users to make informed food choices and track their dietary intake.

5. Community and Sharing: The app features a community platform where users can share baking tips, recipe modifications, and culinary creations with fellow bakers, fostering a sense of community and collaboration among users.

Implementation:

PerfectBake launched the Smart Scale in partnership with culinary influencers and baking enthusiasts, generating buzz and excitement among home bakers. The Smart Scale was promoted through social media campaigns, online tutorials, and live baking demonstrations, highlighting its features and benefits to a wide audience of consumers.

Results:

The PerfectBake Smart Scale received widespread acclaim from both novice and experienced bakers, garnering positive reviews for its ease of use, precision measurement, and recipe assistance features. Sales of the Smart Scale exceeded expectations, with demand surpassing initial projections within the first year of launch. The device has become a staple in kitchens around the world, empowering users to bake with confidence and creativity.

Below is an example of Python code that simulates the functionality of a smart scale for baking. This code allows users to input ingredients and their respective weights, calculates the total weight of the ingredients, and provides a basic recipe based on the ingredients entered.

```python
class SmartScale:
    def __init__(self):
        self.ingredients = {}

    def add_ingredient(self, name, weight):
        self.ingredients[name] = weight

    def calculate_total_weight(self):
        total_weight = sum(self.ingredients.values())
        return total_weight

    def generate_recipe(self):
        total_weight = self.calculate_total_weight()
        if total_weight == 0:
            return "Please add ingredients to generate a recipe."
        elif total_weight < 200:
            return "Mix the ingredients to create a basic dough."
        elif total_weight < 500:
            return "Combine the ingredients to make a cake batter."
        else:
            return "Prepare the ingredients for a hearty loaf of
```

bread."

```
# Example usage
if __name__ == "__main__":
    scale = SmartScale()
    scale.add_ingredient("Flour", 250)
    scale.add_ingredient("Sugar", 150)
    scale.add_ingredient("Butter", 200)

    print("Total          weight          of          ingredients:",
scale.calculate_total_weight())
    print("Recipe suggestion:", scale.generate_recipe())
` ` `
```

This Python code defines a `SmartScale` class with methods to add ingredients, calculate the total weight of ingredients, and generate a basic recipe based on the total weight. In the example usage, we add three ingredients with their respective weights, calculate the total weight, and generate a recipe suggestion based on the total weight of ingredients.

Conclusion:

The PerfectBake Smart Scale has revolutionized the baking experience, providing home bakers with the tools and guidance they need to achieve professional-quality results in the comfort of their own kitchens. By combining precision measurement with intelligent recipe assistance, PerfectBake has empowered users to explore new flavors, experiment with new techniques, and elevate their baking skills to new heights. As a result, the PerfectBake Smart Scale has solidified its position as a must-have kitchen gadget for baking enthusiasts everywhere.

CASE STUDY: CHEFSTEPS JOULE SOUS VIDE - PRECISION COOKING MADE EASY

Background:
ChefSteps is a culinary technology company dedicated to making cooking more accessible and enjoyable for home cooks. In response to the growing popularity of sous vide cooking, ChefSteps developed the Joule Sous Vide, a compact and powerful immersion circulator designed to deliver precise and consistent results in the kitchen.

Challenge:
Sous vide cooking involves cooking food in a precisely controlled water bath at a consistent temperature, resulting in tender, flavorful dishes. However, traditional sous vide equipment can be bulky, complex to operate, and expensive, limiting its accessibility to home cooks. ChefSteps sought to overcome these challenges by developing a sous vide device that is compact, easy to use, and affordable, without compromising on performance or precision.

Solution:
The Joule Sous Vide is a compact and powerful immersion

circulator that brings sous vide cooking to the home kitchen with simplicity and precision. Key features of the Joule Sous Vide include:

1. Compact Design: The Joule Sous Vide is compact and lightweight, making it easy to store and transport, while still delivering powerful performance for precise cooking.

2. Intuitive Interface: The device is controlled via a user-friendly mobile app, which provides step-by-step guidance, temperature control, and recipe recommendations, allowing users to achieve perfect results every time.

3. Powerful Heating Element: The Joule Sous Vide is equipped with a powerful heating element that quickly heats water to the desired temperature and maintains precise temperature control throughout the cooking process, ensuring even and consistent cooking results.

4. Customizable Cooking Settings: The mobile app allows users to customize cooking settings, including time and temperature, to accommodate different types of food and personal preferences, providing flexibility and versatility in the kitchen.

5. Recipe Library: The app features a library of sous vide recipes curated by culinary experts, providing inspiration and guidance for users to explore new flavors and cooking techniques.

Implementation:
ChefSteps launched the Joule Sous Vide with a comprehensive marketing campaign, including social media promotions, cooking demonstrations, and collaborations with culinary influencers. The device was positioned as a game-changer in the home cooking landscape, offering professional-quality results with minimal effort and expertise required.

Results:
The Joule Sous Vide quickly gained popularity among home cooks, receiving rave reviews for its compact design, user-

friendly interface, and precise cooking performance. Sales of the device exceeded expectations, with demand outpacing supply in the months following its launch. The Joule Sous Vide has become a staple in kitchens around the world, empowering users to cook with confidence and precision, whether they're beginners or experienced chefs.

Python Code:

Below is a simplified Python code snippet that simulates the functionality of a sous vide device, allowing users to set the desired temperature and cooking time for sous vide cooking:

```python
class JouleSousVide:
    def __init__(self):
        self.current_temperature = 20  # Default temperature in Celsius
        self.target_temperature = 0
        self.cooking_time = 0

    def set_target_temperature(self, temperature):
        self.target_temperature = temperature

    def set_cooking_time(self, time):
        self.cooking_time = time

    def start_cooking(self):
        print(f"Starting sous vide cooking at {self.target_temperature}°C for {self.cooking_time} minutes.")

# Example usage
if __name__ == "__main__":
    joule = JouleSousVide()
    joule.set_target_temperature(55) # Set target temperature to 55°C
    joule.set_cooking_time(120)    # Set cooking time to 2 hours
    joule.start_cooking()
```

This Python code defines a `JouleSousVide` class with methods to set the target temperature and cooking time for sous vide cooking. In the example usage, we set the target temperature to 55°C and the cooking time to 120 minutes, then start the cooking process. This simulation demonstrates the basic functionality of a sous vide device, allowing users to customize cooking settings and initiate the cooking process with ease.

CASE STUDY: ANOVA PRECISION COOKER - ELEVATING HOME COOKING WITH SOUS VIDE

Background:
Anova Culinary is a leading manufacturer of sous vide immersion circulators, dedicated to democratizing sous vide cooking and empowering home cooks to achieve restaurant-quality results in their own kitchens. The Anova Precision Cooker is a flagship product that combines precision temperature control, user-friendly design, and innovative features to revolutionize the way people cook at home.

Challenge:
Sous vide cooking, while popular among professional chefs, was historically perceived as complicated and inaccessible to home cooks due to the high cost and technical complexity of sous vide equipment. Anova Culinary aimed to overcome these barriers by developing an immersion circulator that is affordable, easy to use, and capable of delivering precise and consistent results for home cooks of all skill levels.

Solution:
The Anova Precision Cooker is an immersion circulator that

attaches to any pot or container, transforming it into a precision cooking device. Key features of the Anova Precision Cooker include:

1. Precision Temperature Control: The device provides precise temperature control within 0.1°C, ensuring consistent cooking results with minimal effort.

2. User-Friendly Interface: The cooker is equipped with a simple interface and a digital display that allows users to easily set the desired temperature and cooking time.

3. Wi-Fi Connectivity: Wi-Fi connectivity enables users to control the cooker remotely via a mobile app, allowing for convenient monitoring and adjustment of cooking settings from anywhere.

4. Recipe Library: The mobile app features a library of sous vide recipes with step-by-step instructions, curated by culinary experts, providing inspiration and guidance for users to explore new dishes and cooking techniques.

5. Multi-Functionality: In addition to sous vide cooking, the Anova Precision Cooker can be used for other cooking methods, such as poaching, steaming, and pasteurizing, enhancing its versatility and value for users.

Implementation:
Anova Culinary launched the Precision Cooker with an extensive marketing campaign targeting home cooks and culinary enthusiasts. The company leveraged social media, influencer partnerships, and cooking demonstrations to showcase the device's features and benefits to a wide audience.

Results:
The Anova Precision Cooker quickly gained traction among home cooks, receiving positive reviews for its affordability, ease of use, and consistent cooking performance. Sales of the device exceeded expectations, with strong demand from both amateur

cooks and seasoned professionals. The Precision Cooker has become a staple in kitchens worldwide, empowering users to explore new culinary possibilities and elevate their cooking skills with precision and confidence.

Python Code:
Below is a simplified Python code snippet that simulates the functionality of a sous vide cooker, allowing users to set the desired temperature and cooking time for sous vide cooking:

```python
class AnovaPrecisionCooker:
    def __init__(self):
        self.current_temperature = 20  # Default temperature in Celsius
        self.target_temperature = 0
        self.cooking_time = 0

    def set_target_temperature(self, temperature):
        self.target_temperature = temperature

    def set_cooking_time(self, time):
        self.cooking_time = time

    def start_cooking(self):
        print(f"Starting sous vide cooking at {self.target_temperature}°C for {self.cooking_time} minutes.")

# Example usage
if __name__ == "__main__":
    anova = AnovaPrecisionCooker()
    anova.set_target_temperature(55)  # Set target temperature to 55°C
    anova.set_cooking_time(120)    # Set cooking time to 2 hours
    anova.start_cooking()
```

This Python code defines an `AnovaPrecisionCooker` class with methods to set the target temperature and cooking time for sous vide cooking. In the example usage, we set the target temperature to 55°C and the cooking time to 120 minutes, then start the cooking process. This simulation demonstrates the basic functionality of a sous vide cooker, allowing users to customize cooking settings and initiate the cooking process with ease.

CASE STUDY: SMART KITCHEN ENERGY MANAGEMENT SYSTEM

Background:
With the increasing focus on sustainability and energy efficiency, smart kitchen technology is playing a crucial role in helping users reduce power consumption and minimize their environmental footprint. This case study explores how a smart kitchen energy management system can leverage data analytics and automation to optimize energy usage and reduce electricity costs.

Challenge:
Traditional kitchen appliances consume significant amounts of energy, contributing to high electricity bills and environmental impact. However, with the integration of smart sensors, IoT devices, and machine learning algorithms, there is an opportunity to monitor and control energy usage in real-time, identifying inefficiencies and implementing energy-saving measures proactively.

Solution:
A smart kitchen energy management system can consist of various components, including smart appliances, energy monitoring devices, and a central control hub. Key features of

the system may include:

1. Appliance Monitoring: Smart sensors installed in kitchen appliances monitor energy consumption, usage patterns, and operating efficiency in real-time.

2. Energy Analytics: Data analytics algorithms analyze energy usage data to identify trends, patterns, and inefficiencies, providing insights into areas for optimization.

3. Automated Control: Based on energy analytics insights, the system can automatically adjust appliance settings, such as temperature, power levels, and operating schedules, to minimize energy waste and optimize efficiency.

4. User Interface: A user-friendly interface, such as a mobile app or web dashboard, allows users to monitor energy usage, set preferences, and receive recommendations for energy-saving actions.

Implementation:
To demonstrate the concept of a smart kitchen energy management system, we can create a simple Python script that simulates energy monitoring and optimization for a set of virtual appliances. The script will monitor the energy usage of each appliance and implement energy-saving measures based on predefined rules and thresholds.

Python Code:

```python
class SmartAppliance:
    def __init__(self, name):
        self.name = name
        self.power_consumption = 0

    def update_power_consumption(self, power):
        self.power_consumption = power

class EnergyManagementSystem:
```

```python
    def __init__(self):
        self.appliances = []

    def add_appliance(self, appliance):
        self.appliances.append(appliance)

    def monitor_energy_usage(self):
        total_power_consumption = sum(appliance.power_consumption for appliance in self.appliances)
        print(f"Total energy usage: {total_power_consumption} kWh")

    def optimize_energy_usage(self):
        # Example: Turn off appliances with low power consumption
        for appliance in self.appliances:
            if appliance.power_consumption < 10: # Threshold for turning off appliance (in watts)
                print(f"Turning off {appliance.name} to save energy")

# Example usage
if __name__ == "__main__":
    # Create smart appliances
    oven = SmartAppliance("Oven")
    refrigerator = SmartAppliance("Refrigerator")
    dishwasher = SmartAppliance("Dishwasher")

    # Create energy management system
    energy_system = EnergyManagementSystem()

    # Add appliances to energy management system
    energy_system.add_appliance(oven)
    energy_system.add_appliance(refrigerator)
    energy_system.add_appliance(dishwasher)

    # Simulate energy monitoring and optimization
    oven.update_power_consumption(1000)    # Update power
```

consumption for oven (in watts)

```
    refrigerator.update_power_consumption(200)      # Update
power consumption for refrigerator
    dishwasher.update_power_consumption(500)      # Update
power consumption for dishwasher

    energy_system.monitor_energy_usage()
    energy_system.optimize_energy_usage()
` ` `
```

This Python code simulates a simple smart kitchen energy management system with three virtual appliances: oven, refrigerator, and dishwasher. The script monitors the energy usage of each appliance and implements energy-saving measures, such as turning off appliances with low power consumption, to optimize energy usage in the kitchen. While this is a basic example, a real-world smart kitchen energy management system would incorporate more sophisticated algorithms and automation features to achieve greater energy efficiency and cost savings.

CASE STUDY: SMART LIGHTING CONTROL IN THE KITCHEN

Background:
Lighting is a significant contributor to energy consumption in households, including the kitchen. Traditional lighting systems often result in unnecessary energy usage due to inefficient controls and lack of automation. This case study explores how smart lighting control solutions can optimize energy usage in the kitchen while enhancing convenience and comfort for users.

Challenge:
The challenge lies in reducing energy wastage associated with lighting in the kitchen without compromising visibility, safety, or usability. Traditional lighting systems often rely on manual control or basic timers, which may lead to lights being left on unnecessarily or inadequate lighting levels for various tasks.

Solution:
A smart lighting control system for the kitchen offers several features to address energy efficiency and user convenience:

1. Motion Sensors: Installing motion sensors in the kitchen allows lights to automatically turn on when someone enters the room and turn off when the room is unoccupied, reducing energy waste from lights being left on unnecessarily.

2. Dimmable Lighting: Dimmable LED bulbs or fixtures can

adjust the brightness level based on the time of day or specific activities, providing adequate lighting while minimizing energy consumption.

3. Schedule and Scene Settings: Users can create custom schedules or scenes for different times of the day or activities, such as cooking, dining, or cleaning, to ensure appropriate lighting levels and energy efficiency.

4. Remote Control and Automation: Integration with smart home platforms or mobile apps enables users to control lighting remotely and set automation rules based on triggers such as sunset/sunrise or occupancy, optimizing energy usage and convenience.

Implementation:
To illustrate the benefits of a smart lighting control system in the kitchen, we can create a Python script that simulates motion-activated lighting control and dimming functionality.

Python Code:

```python
class SmartLightingSystem:
    def __init__(self):
        self.motion_sensor = False
        self.light_brightness = 0

    def detect_motion(self):
        self.motion_sensor = True
        print("Motion detected in the kitchen.")

    def adjust_light_brightness(self, brightness):
        self.light_brightness = brightness
        print(f"Adjusting light brightness to {brightness}%.")

# Example usage
if __name__ == "__main__":
    kitchen_lights = SmartLightingSystem()
```

```
# Simulate motion detection triggering lighting control
kitchen_lights.detect_motion()

# Simulate adjusting light brightness based on time of day
if kitchen_lights.motion_sensor:
    # Daytime brightness settings
    kitchen_lights.adjust_light_brightness(100)
else:
    # Nighttime or unoccupied settings
    kitchen_lights.adjust_light_brightness(50)
```

This Python code simulates a smart lighting system for the kitchen with motion detection and brightness adjustment functionality. When motion is detected in the kitchen, the script adjusts the light brightness accordingly, simulating the system's response to occupancy and optimizing energy usage based on the time of day or activity level. While this is a basic example, a real-world smart lighting control system would incorporate more advanced features and integration with sensors, schedules, and user preferences to achieve greater energy efficiency and user satisfaction.

CASE STUDY: SMART KITCHEN APPLIANCES AND PEAK ENERGY MANAGEMENT

Background:
Peak energy demand during certain times of the day can strain electrical grids and increase energy costs for consumers. Kitchen appliances, such as ovens, stoves, and dishwashers, contribute to peak demand when used simultaneously during peak hours. This case study explores how smart kitchen appliances can help manage peak energy demand through load shifting and scheduling.

Challenge:
The challenge lies in reducing peak energy demand in residential kitchens without sacrificing user convenience or comfort. Traditional kitchen appliances operate independently, leading to simultaneous energy consumption during peak hours, which strains the grid and increases energy costs for consumers.

Solution:
Smart kitchen appliances equipped with scheduling and energy management features offer a solution to peak energy demand management:

1. Load Shifting: Appliances can be programmed to operate during off-peak hours when energy demand and costs are lower, reducing strain on the grid and saving consumers money.

2. Energy Monitoring: Built-in energy monitoring capabilities allow appliances to track energy usage in real-time, providing insights into consumption patterns and identifying opportunities for optimization.

3. Smart Scheduling: Users can schedule appliance operations based on their preferences and energy tariffs, ensuring efficient use of energy resources and minimizing peak demand.

4. Remote Control: Integration with smart home platforms or mobile apps enables users to monitor and control appliances remotely, allowing for flexibility and convenience in managing energy usage.

Implementation:
To demonstrate the benefits of smart kitchen appliances for peak energy management, we can create a Python script that simulates scheduling and energy monitoring functionality.

Python Code:

```python
class SmartKitchenAppliance:
    def __init__(self, name):
        self.name = name
        self.scheduled_start_time = None
        self.energy_usage = 0

    def set_schedule(self, start_time):
        self.scheduled_start_time = start_time
        print(f"{self.name} scheduled to start at {start_time}.")

    def start_appliance(self):
        if self.scheduled_start_time:
            print(f"{self.name}            starting            at
```

```
{self.scheduled_start_time}.")
        # Simulate energy usage during operation
        self.energy_usage += 100  # Example energy usage in
watts
    else:
        print(f"No schedule set for {self.name}.")

    def get_energy_usage(self):
        print(f"Total    energy    usage    for    {self.name}:
{self.energy_usage} Wh.")

# Example usage
if __name__ == "__main__":
    oven = SmartKitchenAppliance("Oven")
    dishwasher = SmartKitchenAppliance("Dishwasher")

    # Set schedules for appliances
    oven.set_schedule("10:00 AM")
    dishwasher.set_schedule("11:00 AM")

    # Start appliances based on schedule
    oven.start_appliance()
    dishwasher.start_appliance()

    # Monitor energy usage
    oven.get_energy_usage()
    dishwasher.get_energy_usage()
```

This Python code simulates smart kitchen appliances with scheduling and energy monitoring functionality. Appliances are scheduled to start at specific times, allowing for load shifting and optimization of energy usage. Users can monitor energy usage to track consumption patterns and identify opportunities for further optimization. While this is a simplified example, real-world smart kitchen appliances would incorporate more advanced features and integration with energy management systems to achieve peak demand management and energy savings.

CASE STUDY: SMART KITCHEN WATER MANAGEMENT SYSTEM

Background:
Water scarcity and conservation are pressing environmental concerns, and the kitchen is one of the areas where significant water usage occurs. This case study explores how smart kitchen technology can contribute to reducing water consumption through monitoring, automation, and efficiency optimization.

Challenge:
Traditional kitchen appliances, such as faucets, dishwashers, and refrigerators, often waste water due to inefficient usage patterns and lack of monitoring capabilities. Addressing this challenge requires the implementation of smart solutions that can track water usage, detect leaks, and optimize water flow to minimize waste.

Solution:
A smart kitchen water management system offers several features to address water conservation challenges:

1. Water Usage Monitoring: Smart sensors installed in faucets, dishwashers, and other water-using appliances monitor water consumption in real-time, providing insights into usage

patterns and identifying areas for improvement.

2. Leak Detection: Advanced leak detection algorithms analyze water flow data to detect leaks or abnormal usage patterns, enabling timely intervention to prevent water wastage and minimize damage.

3. Automated Flow Control: Smart faucets and dishwashers can adjust water flow based on usage requirements, optimizing water usage while maintaining usability and convenience for users.

4. Usage Insights and Recommendations: Integration with mobile apps or dashboards allows users to track water usage, receive alerts for potential leaks or wastage, and access personalized recommendations for reducing water consumption.

Implementation:
To illustrate the benefits of a smart kitchen water management system, we can create a Python script that simulates water usage monitoring, leak detection, and automated flow control for a virtual kitchen environment.

Python Code:

```python
class SmartFaucet:
    def __init__(self):
        self.water_flow_rate = 0
        self.leak_detected = False

    def set_water_flow_rate(self, flow_rate):
        self.water_flow_rate = flow_rate

    def detect_leak(self):
        if self.water_flow_rate > 0:
            self.leak_detected = True
            print("Leak detected in the faucet. Shutting off water
```

flow.")

```python
    def adjust_flow_rate(self):
        if self.leak_detected:
            print("Leak detected. Adjusting flow rate to minimize water wastage.")
            self.water_flow_rate = 0
        else:
            print("No leaks detected. Maintaining normal flow rate.")

# Example usage
if __name__ == "__main__":
    kitchen_faucet = SmartFaucet()

    # Simulate water flow and leak detection
    kitchen_faucet.set_water_flow_rate(0.5)   # Set water flow rate (in gallons per minute)
    kitchen_faucet.detect_leak()

    # Adjust flow rate based on leak detection
    kitchen_faucet.adjust_flow_rate()
```
```

This Python code simulates a smart faucet with water flow monitoring, leak detection, and automated flow control functionality. The script sets the water flow rate, simulates leak detection based on the flow rate, and adjusts the flow rate accordingly to minimize water wastage in case of a leak. While this is a basic example, real-world smart kitchen water management systems would incorporate more sophisticated sensors, algorithms, and integration with appliances to achieve greater water conservation and efficiency.
```

CASE STUDY: SMART KITCHEN FOOD WASTAGE REDUCTION SYSTEM

Background:
Food wastage is a significant issue globally, with a significant portion of waste occurring in households. Smart kitchen technology offers an opportunity to address this challenge by providing users with real-time information and recommendations to reduce food wastage. This case study explores how a smart kitchen system can help users minimize food wastage by prompting them to cook particular food items before they expire.

Challenge:
One of the main challenges in reducing food wastage is identifying and utilizing perishable food items before they spoil. Many households struggle with managing their food inventory effectively, leading to items being forgotten or overlooked until they are no longer usable. Addressing this challenge requires a solution that can track food inventory, monitor expiration dates, and provide timely recommendations for using or preserving perishable items.

Solution:
A smart kitchen food wastage reduction system offers several

features to help users manage their food inventory and minimize wastage:

1. Inventory Tracking: The system tracks the user's food inventory, including perishable items such as fruits, vegetables, dairy, and meat products.

2. Expiration Date Monitoring: The system monitors the expiration dates of perishable items and sends alerts or notifications to the user when items are approaching their expiration dates.

3. Recipe Recommendation: Based on the user's inventory and expiration dates, the system recommends recipes that utilize perishable items that are nearing their expiration dates, encouraging users to cook or consume them before they spoil.

4. Customization and Flexibility: Users can customize their preferences, dietary restrictions, and cooking preferences to receive personalized recommendations that align with their tastes and lifestyle.

Implementation:
To illustrate the benefits of a smart kitchen food wastage reduction system, we can create a Python script that simulates inventory tracking, expiration date monitoring, and recipe recommendation functionality for a virtual kitchen environment.

Python Code:

```python
class SmartKitchenSystem:
    def __init__(self):
        self.inventory = {}

    def add_item(self, item, expiration_date):
        self.inventory[item] = expiration_date

    def check_expiration_dates(self):
```

```
    for item, expiration_date in self.inventory.items():
        if expiration_date <= 0:
            print(f"{item} has expired. Please discard it.")
        elif expiration_date <= 3:
            print(f"{item} is expiring soon. Consider cooking it.")
        else:
            print(f"{item} is still fresh.")

    def recommend_recipe(self):
        for item, expiration_date in self.inventory.items():
            if expiration_date <= 3:
                print(f"Recommended recipe for {item}: Stir-fry with
{item} and vegetables.")
            else:
                print(f"No recommended recipe for {item} at this
time.")

# Example usage
if __name__ == "__main__":
    kitchen_system = SmartKitchenSystem()

    # Add items to inventory with expiration dates (in days)
    kitchen_system.add_item("Chicken", 2)
    kitchen_system.add_item("Spinach", 5)
    kitchen_system.add_item("Milk", 1)

    # Check expiration dates and recommend recipes
    kitchen_system.check_expiration_dates()
    kitchen_system.recommend_recipe()
```

This Python code simulates a smart kitchen system with inventory tracking, expiration date monitoring, and recipe recommendation functionality. The script adds items to the inventory with expiration dates, checks the expiration dates, and recommends recipes for items that are nearing their expiration dates. While this is a basic example, real-world smart kitchen food wastage reduction systems would incorporate more advanced features, such as barcode scanning, integration with grocery lists, and machine learning algorithms, to provide more accurate and personalized recommendations for users.

CASE STUDY: SMART KITCHEN INVENTORY MANAGEMENT SYSTEM

Background:
Efficient management of kitchen inventory is essential for minimizing waste, optimizing meal planning, and ensuring ingredients are readily available when needed. However, traditional methods of inventory management can be tedious and prone to errors. This case study explores how a smart kitchen inventory management system can streamline the process, reduce waste, and enhance overall efficiency.

Challenge:
The main challenge in kitchen inventory management is keeping track of the items on hand, their quantities, and their expiration dates. Many households struggle with overstocking, leading to food waste, or understocking, resulting in last-minute trips to the grocery store. Addressing this challenge requires a solution that can accurately track inventory levels, monitor expiration dates, and provide timely recommendations for restocking or using items before they expire.

Solution:
A smart kitchen inventory management system offers several features to help users track, manage, and optimize their kitchen

inventory:

1. Barcode Scanning: Users can scan barcodes or manually input items into the system to add them to the inventory, streamlining the process and reducing errors.

2. Inventory Tracking: The system maintains a real-time inventory of items on hand, including quantities, expiration dates, and location within the kitchen.

3. Expiration Date Monitoring: The system monitors expiration dates of perishable items and sends alerts or notifications when items are approaching their expiration dates, prompting users to use or restock them.

4. Recipe Integration: Integration with recipe databases allows the system to suggest recipes based on available ingredients, helping users make use of items before they expire and reducing waste.

Implementation:
To illustrate the benefits of a smart kitchen inventory management system, we can create a Python script that simulates inventory tracking, expiration date monitoring, and recipe integration functionality for a virtual kitchen environment.

Python Code:

```python
class SmartInventoryManagementSystem:
    def __init__(self):
        self.inventory = {}

    def add_item(self, item, quantity, expiration_date):
        if item in self.inventory:
            self.inventory[item]["quantity"] += quantity
        else:
            self.inventory[item]      =      {"quantity":      quantity,
```

```
"expiration_date": expiration_date}

    def check_expiration_dates(self):
        for item, details in self.inventory.items():
            if details["expiration_date"] <= 0:
                print(f"{item} has expired. Please discard it.")
            elif details["expiration_date"] <= 3:
                print(f"{item} is expiring soon. Consider using it.")
            else:
                print(f"{item} is still fresh.")

    def suggest_recipe(self):
        # Example: Suggest recipe based on available ingredients
        available_items = [item for item, details in
self.inventory.items() if details["quantity"] > 0]
        if available_items:
            print(f"Recommended recipe: Pasta with {',
'.join(available_items)}.")
        else:
            print("No recommended recipe. Inventory is empty.")

# Example usage
if __name__ == "__main__":
    inventory_system = SmartInventoryManagementSystem()

    # Add items to inventory with quantities and expiration
dates (in days)
    inventory_system.add_item("Pasta", 1, 5)
    inventory_system.add_item("Tomato Sauce", 2, 10)
    inventory_system.add_item("Spinach", 1, 2)

    # Check expiration dates and suggest recipes
    inventory_system.check_expiration_dates()
    inventory_system.suggest_recipe()
` ` `
```

This Python code simulates a smart kitchen inventory management system with inventory tracking, expiration date monitoring, and recipe integration functionality. The script adds items to the inventory with quantities and expiration dates, checks the expiration dates, and suggests a recipe based on available ingredients. While this is a basic example, real-world smart kitchen inventory management systems would incorporate more advanced features, such as barcode scanning, integration with grocery lists, and machine learning algorithms, to provide more accurate and personalized recommendations for users.

CASE STUDY: ENERGY-EFFICIENT COOKING WITH COMPUTER VISION IN SMART KITCHENS

Background:
Smart kitchen technology has the potential to revolutionize energy efficiency by leveraging computer vision to optimize cooking processes. This case study explores how computer vision can be integrated into smart kitchen appliances to reduce energy consumption while enhancing cooking performance and user experience.

Challenge:
Traditional cooking methods often involve inefficiencies in energy usage, such as preheating ovens for longer than necessary or using excessive heat during stovetop cooking. Addressing these challenges requires a solution that can accurately monitor cooking processes in real-time, adjust settings dynamically based on visual cues, and optimize energy usage without compromising cooking performance.

Solution:
A smart kitchen system with computer vision capabilities offers several energy-efficient approaches to cooking:

1. Optimized Cooking Settings: Computer vision algorithms analyze visual data from cooking processes to determine optimal settings such as temperature, cooking time, and power level, minimizing energy waste while ensuring food is cooked to perfection.

2. Precise Heat Control: Smart stovetops and ovens equipped with computer vision can adjust heat output based on the size, shape, and composition of cookware and ingredients, reducing energy consumption and improving cooking efficiency.

3. Energy Monitoring and Feedback: Real-time energy monitoring and feedback mechanisms provide users with insights into energy usage during cooking, encouraging mindful consumption habits and promoting energy conservation.

4. Adaptive Cooking Assistance: Computer vision-enabled cooking assistants provide users with real-time guidance and feedback on cooking techniques, ingredient proportions, and recipe execution, helping optimize energy usage and improve cooking outcomes.

Implementation:
To demonstrate the benefits of energy-efficient cooking with computer vision in smart kitchens, we can create a Python script that simulates a computer vision-enabled cooking process and adjusts cooking settings based on visual cues.

Python Code:

```python
class SmartCookingSystem:
    def __init__(self):
        self.cooking_status = "Idle"
        self.energy_usage = 0

    def start_cooking(self, recipe):
        print(f"Starting cooking: {recipe}")
```

```
        self.cooking_status = "Active"

    def adjust_heat(self, visual_data):
        # Example: Adjust heat based on visual cues from
computer vision
        if "boiling" in visual_data:
            print("Water is boiling. Lowering heat to maintain
simmer.")
        elif "grilling" in visual_data:
            print("Grilling detected. Increasing heat for searing.")
        else:
            print("No specific cooking action detected. Maintaining
current heat level.")

    def monitor_energy_usage(self):
        # Example: Simulate energy usage during cooking process
        self.energy_usage += 100 # Example energy usage in watts
        print(f"Total     energy     usage     during     cooking:
{self.energy_usage} Wh.")

# Example usage
if __name__ == "__main__":
    cooking_system = SmartCookingSystem()

    # Simulate start of cooking process
    cooking_system.start_cooking("Grilled Salmon")

    # Simulate computer vision analysis of cooking process
    visual_data = ["grilling", "sizzling"]
    cooking_system.adjust_heat(visual_data)

    # Monitor energy usage during cooking
    cooking_system.monitor_energy_usage()
```

This Python code simulates a smart cooking system with computer vision capabilities that adjust cooking settings based on visual cues detected during the cooking process. The script starts the cooking process, analyzes visual data from computer vision, adjusts heat settings accordingly, and monitors energy usage throughout the cooking process. While this is a basic example, real-world smart kitchen systems would incorporate more advanced computer vision algorithms and integration with smart appliances to achieve greater energy efficiency and cooking performance.

CASE STUDY: MACHINE LEARNING-BASED PURCHASE OPTIMIZATION FOR SMART KITCHENS

Background:
Managing grocery shopping efficiently is crucial for maintaining a well-stocked kitchen while minimizing waste and ensuring freshness. Machine learning algorithms can analyze various factors such as consumption patterns, ingredient availability, and expiration dates to optimize the timing of purchasing specific items for the kitchen. This case study explores how machine learning can be leveraged to recommend the ideal timing for purchasing particular items based on individual user preferences and habits.

Challenge:
The challenge lies in predicting the optimal timing for purchasing specific items to ensure they are available when needed without overstocking or allowing items to spoil. Traditional approaches to grocery shopping may rely on fixed schedules or manual estimation, leading to inefficiencies and waste. Addressing this challenge requires a solution that can analyze historical data, identify patterns and trends, and

generate personalized recommendations for purchasing specific items at the right time.

Solution:
A machine learning-based purchase optimization system for smart kitchens offers several benefits:

1. Personalized Recommendations: Machine learning algorithms analyze individual user data, including consumption patterns, meal preferences, and inventory levels, to generate personalized recommendations for purchasing specific items at the optimal time.

2. Predictive Analytics: By analyzing historical data and external factors such as seasonality and weather patterns, machine learning models can predict future demand for specific items and recommend purchasing strategies to minimize waste and ensure availability.

3. Dynamic Adjustment: The system continuously learns and adapts to changes in user behavior, preferences, and external factors, allowing it to dynamically adjust recommendations and optimize purchasing decisions over time.

4. Integration with Smart Devices: Integration with smart kitchen appliances and grocery delivery services enables seamless execution of recommended purchasing strategies, enhancing convenience and user experience.

Implementation:
To demonstrate the benefits of machine learning-based purchase optimization for smart kitchens, we can create a Python script that simulates a recommendation system for purchasing specific items based on historical data and user preferences.

Python Code:

```python
```

```python
import numpy as np
from sklearn.linear_model import LinearRegression

class PurchaseOptimizationSystem:
    def __init__(self):
        # Initialize machine learning model
        self.model = LinearRegression()

    def train_model(self, historical_data, target_data):
        # Train machine learning model
        self.model.fit(historical_data, target_data)

    def predict_purchase_timing(self, user_preferences):
        # Example: Predict optimal timing for purchasing specific
items based on user preferences
        predicted_timing = self.model.predict(user_preferences)
        return predicted_timing

# Example usage
if __name__ == "__main__":
    purchase_system = PurchaseOptimizationSystem()

    # Example historical data (e.g., user's past purchases,
consumption patterns)
    historical_data = np.array([[1, 2, 3], [4, 5, 6], [7, 8, 9]])  #
Example features
    target_data = np.array([10, 20, 30]) # Example target variable
(optimal purchase timing)

    # Train machine learning model
    purchase_system.train_model(historical_data, target_data)

    # Example user preferences (e.g., current inventory levels,
meal plans)
    user_preferences = np.array([[3, 2, 1]]) # Example features for
user preferences

    # Predict optimal timing for purchasing specific items based
on user preferences
```

```
    predicted_timing                                    =
purchase_system.predict_purchase_timing(user_preferences)
    print("Predicted optimal timing for purchasing specific
items:", predicted_timing)
```

This Python code simulates a machine learning-based purchase optimization system for smart kitchens. The script trains a linear regression model using historical data on past purchases and consumption patterns, then predicts the optimal timing for purchasing specific items based on user preferences. While this is a basic example, real-world purchase optimization systems would incorporate more advanced machine learning algorithms, larger datasets, and integration with smart devices and external data sources to provide more accurate and personalized recommendations for users.

CASE STUDY: WASTE REDUCTION THROUGH PREDICTIVE INVENTORY MANAGEMENT IN SMART KITCHENS

Background:
One of the significant challenges in kitchen management is minimizing food waste while ensuring that essential ingredients are always available. This case study explores how predictive analytics can be employed in smart kitchens to optimize inventory levels, reduce waste, and ensure that ingredients are replenished just in time.

Challenge:
The challenge lies in accurately predicting future consumption patterns and inventory needs while considering factors such as ingredient shelf life, meal planning, and seasonal variations. Traditional inventory management methods often rely on manual estimation or fixed schedules, which can lead to

overstocking, waste, or shortages. Addressing this challenge requires a solution that can analyze historical data, anticipate future demand, and dynamically adjust inventory levels to optimize usage and minimize waste.

Solution:
A predictive inventory management system for smart kitchens offers several benefits:

1. Data Analysis: By analyzing historical consumption patterns, meal plans, and ingredient usage, predictive analytics algorithms can identify trends and patterns to forecast future demand accurately.

2. Dynamic Inventory Optimization: Based on predictive models, the system can dynamically adjust inventory levels, ensuring that ingredients are replenished just in time to meet anticipated demand without overstocking or waste.

3. Shelf Life Monitoring: Integrating shelf life data into predictive models allows the system to prioritize ingredients nearing expiration and recommend using them before they spoil, minimizing waste.

4. Integration with Suppliers: Integration with grocery delivery services or suppliers enables seamless replenishment of inventory based on predictive recommendations, ensuring that essential ingredients are always available when needed.

Implementation:
To demonstrate the benefits of predictive inventory management in smart kitchens, we can create a Python script that simulates a predictive model for forecasting ingredient demand and optimizing inventory levels.

Python Code:

```python
import numpy as np
```

```python
from sklearn.linear_model import LinearRegression

class PredictiveInventoryManagementSystem:
    def __init__(self):
        # Initialize machine learning model
        self.model = LinearRegression()

    def train_model(self, historical_data, target_data):
        # Train machine learning model
        self.model.fit(historical_data, target_data)

    def predict_inventory_levels(self, future_demand):
        # Example: Predict optimal inventory levels based on
forecasted demand
        predicted_inventory = self.model.predict(future_demand)
        return predicted_inventory

# Example usage
if __name__ == "__main__":
    inventory_system                                         =
PredictiveInventoryManagementSystem()

    # Example historical data (e.g., past consumption patterns,
meal plans)
    historical_data = np.array([[1, 2, 3], [4, 5, 6], [7, 8, 9]])  #
Example features
    target_data = np.array([10, 20, 30]) # Example target variable
(future inventory levels)

    # Train machine learning model
    inventory_system.train_model(historical_data, target_data)

    # Example future demand forecast
    future_demand = np.array([[3, 2, 1]]) # Example features for
future demand

    # Predict optimal inventory levels based on forecasted
demand
    predicted_inventory                                      =
```

```
inventory_system.predict_inventory_levels(future_demand)
    print("Predicted       optimal       inventory       levels:",
predicted_inventory)
```
```

This Python code simulates a predictive inventory management system for smart kitchens. The script trains a linear regression model using historical data on past consumption patterns and meal plans, then predicts optimal inventory levels based on forecasted demand. While this is a basic example, real-world predictive inventory management systems would incorporate more advanced machine learning algorithms, larger datasets, and integration with suppliers and delivery services to provide more accurate and timely recommendations for users.
```

CASE STUDY: POLLUTION REDUCTION THROUGH ENERGY-EFFICIENT SMART KITCHENS

Background:
Traditional kitchen appliances contribute to indoor air pollution through the emission of greenhouse gases and other harmful pollutants. Smart kitchens equipped with energy-efficient appliances and advanced ventilation systems offer an opportunity to mitigate pollution while improving energy efficiency and indoor air quality. This case study explores how smart kitchens can reduce pollution through energy-efficient practices and technologies.

Challenge:
Indoor air pollution in kitchens is primarily caused by cooking activities, particularly those involving gas stoves or inefficient appliances. Addressing this challenge requires a solution that can minimize emissions from cooking, improve ventilation to remove pollutants, and promote energy-efficient practices to reduce overall pollution levels.

Solution:
A pollution reduction strategy for smart kitchens focuses on the following key areas:

1. Energy-Efficient Appliances: Upgrading to energy-efficient appliances, such as induction cooktops and convection ovens, reduces energy consumption and emissions while maintaining cooking performance.

2. Advanced Ventilation Systems: Installing advanced ventilation systems, such as range hoods with high-efficiency filters and smart exhaust fans, removes pollutants and odors from the air, improving indoor air quality.

3. Pollution Monitoring: Integrating pollution monitoring sensors into smart kitchens allows users to track pollutant levels in real-time and adjust ventilation settings accordingly to minimize exposure.

4. Behavioral Changes: Promoting energy-efficient cooking practices, such as using lids on pots and pans, cooking with smaller appliances when possible, and avoiding overcooking, further reduces emissions and pollution levels.

Implementation:
To demonstrate the pollution reduction benefits of energy-efficient smart kitchens, we can create a Python script that simulates the impact of upgrading to energy-efficient appliances and implementing advanced ventilation systems on indoor air quality.

Python Code:

```python
class PollutionReductionSystem:
    def __init__(self):
        self.energy_savings = 0
        self.pollutant_reduction = 0
```

```python
    def calculate_energy_savings(self, old_appliance_energy,
new_appliance_energy, cooking_time):
        # Calculate energy savings from upgrading to energy-
efficient appliances
        energy_saved_per_use  =  old_appliance_energy  -
new_appliance_energy
        self.energy_savings  =  energy_saved_per_use  *
cooking_time

    def                 calculate_pollutant_reduction(self,
pollutant_emission_rate, cooking_time):
        # Calculate pollutant reduction based on energy savings
and emission rate
        self.pollutant_reduction  =  pollutant_emission_rate  *
self.energy_savings / cooking_time

# Example usage
if __name__ == "__main__":
    pollution_system = PollutionReductionSystem()

    # Example parameters
    old_appliance_energy = 1000  # Energy consumption of old
appliance (in watts)
    new_appliance_energy = 500  # Energy consumption of new
energy-efficient appliance (in watts)
    cooking_time = 30  # Cooking time (in minutes)
    pollutant_emission_rate = 0.05  # Pollutant emission rate (in
grams per watt-hour)

    # Calculate energy savings and pollutant reduction
    pollution_system.calculate_energy_savings(old_appliance_e
nergy, new_appliance_energy, cooking_time)
    pollution_system.calculate_pollutant_reduction(pollutant_e
mission_rate, cooking_time)

    # Print results
    print("Energy savings:", pollution_system.energy_savings,
```

```
"watt-hours")
    print("Pollutant                                    reduction:",
pollution_system.pollutant_reduction, "grams")
    ` ` `
```

This Python code simulates a pollution reduction system for smart kitchens by calculating the energy savings and pollutant reduction achieved through upgrading to energy-efficient appliances and reducing cooking time. While this is a basic example, real-world pollution reduction strategies would consider additional factors such as ventilation efficiency, pollutant types, and user behavior to achieve greater indoor air quality improvements and pollution reduction benefits.

www.ingramcontent.com/pod-product-compliance
Lightning Source LLC
Chambersburg PA
CBHW071250050326
40690CB00011B/2336